Transform the Coal in your Soul to Diamonds

How to Become a Leadership King by Polishing Yourself Right Up to the Top

Vince Labossiere
Award Winning Author

Transform the Coal in your Soul to Diamonds
How to Become a Leadership King by Polishing Yourself
Right up to the Top

Copyright © 2017 by Vince Labossiere

ISBN-13: 978-1981879687
ISBN-10: 1981879684

No part of this publication may be reproduced, stored in a retrieval system or transmitted in any form or by any means, electronic, mechanical, photocopying, recording, scanning or otherwise.

All rights reserved, including the right to reproduce this book or portions thereof in any form whatsoever.

Published by:
10-10-10 Publishing

First 10-10-10 Publishing paperback edition December 2017

Contents

Foreword	ix
Acknowledgements	xi
Chapter 1: How Old is Your Coal?	**1**
What Fuel Are You Using?	1
Is Soul Coal a "Fossil Fuel?"	3
Stresses to Your Soul	6
Does Age Matter?	9
Energy Efficiency	11
Evolution = Evolve + Solution	14
Chapter 2: Failing Victories	**17**
Fail to Win	17
Where Do You Rank?	19
Strip Down to the Core	21
Name Your Competition	24
Emotional Training	26
Every Session Counts	29
Chapter 3: Value of Soul Diamonds	**33**
Scarcity Creates Highest Value	33
The Most Abrasive Mineral in the World	35
Mine Your Soul	37
Sharp Defined Edges	40
Mirrored Prism	42
Unlimited Resource	44

Chapter 4: Where to find a Leadership Polishing Kit — 47
Polishing Soul Coal into Soul Diamonds — 47
Become a Chemist — 49
Open Up Your Own M.I.N.E.ing Company — 51
Become a Polishing Apprentice — 54
Polish it....and They Will Come — 56
Invest to Obtain the Top Leadership Polishing Kit — 58

Chapter 5: Follow the Leader? — 63
What is Your Title? — 63
Push or Pull? — 66
To Be or Not to Be....Isn't That the Real Question? — 68
Earn the Right — 70
Minimum of 2 Choices — 73
Inside Out — 74

Chapter 6: ProActive = ActivePro — 77
Become a Solution Specialist — 77
Practice Practicing and Become a Pro — 79
Aerodynamic Theory — 82
Inertia Overhaul — 85
Present Yourself with a....Present! — 87
Which league are you playing in? — 89

Chapter 7: Leadership is for the Birds — 91
Who's Leading? — 91
It's Not Only About the "I", It's About the "V"! — 93
Birds of a Feather DO Flock Together — 96
Communication Stimulation — 98
Does the Early Bird *Really* Get the Worm? — 102
Maximize Your Flight Plan — 104

Transform the Coal in your Soul to Diamonds

Chapter 8: Nature's Patterned Secrets	**109**
It's a Bird, It's a Plane, It's.....a Pattern?	109
Assembling the Assembly Line	112
Succeed with Speed from the Seed	114
Human Automation	116
What Would Darwin Think?	118
Create Your Own Pattern	119
Chapter 9: Captainship is Today's Leadership King	**123**
Captain + Ship = Captainship	123
First One On....Last One Off	125
Disciplined Responsibility	127
Trusting Confidence	129
GPS Your Path	131
Captain's Crown	132
Chapter 10: Shine Bright Like a Diamond	**135**
Blissful Reflections	135
Glowing Rheostatic Intensity	137
Symbol of Commitment	138
Propose to Yourself	140
Infinite Value	142
Is it I'm-possible that d-I-AM-ond's are Forever?	144
About the Author	147

I dedicate this book to my dad. He always guided me to take action so as to strip away the inefficiencies of failures, and polish myself towards achieving the greatest heights of my deepest dreams and desires.

Foreword

There is absolutely no way you will not feel a changed person after reading this book. It contains multiple examples and strategies to help you overcome obstacles, to thereby allow yourself to shine brightly. Book your own voyage by reading this book, *Transform the Coal in your Soul to Diamonds*, and strip away the inefficiencies of your past in order to unearth your internal diamonds for the future!

I am impressed with Vince's methodology and metaphorical references. It doesn't happen often where a book destabilizes me. So, when he told me about *Transform the Coal in your Soul to Diamonds*, I promptly acknowledged the interconnection between this illustrious, profound work and how Vince can metamorphosis your inner core.

I was first introduced to Vince at a private luncheon through Lisa, who happens to be the mother of my daughter Emma. I was immediately drawn into his uncanny ability to create a compelling rapport and mesmerized by his ability to passionately connect with others. Experience his aptitude for creating empathetic affinities with your innermost spiritedness to transform your life.

I am a New York Times Bestselling Author and have been publishing for quite some time now, so when Vince Labossiere shared his ideas with me, I eagerly committed to wanting to publish his work.

Transform the Coal in your Soul to Diamonds

I highly recommend Vince's book as an absolute must read and one that should be gifted to others. What makes this book so captivating is that it allows you to start where you currently are and take immediate action in order to alter your transformation to the top level. What an incredible expedition!

I enthusiastically recommend Vince and Transform the *Coal in your Soul to Diamonds!*

Raymond Aaron
New York Times Bestselling Author

Acknowledgements

I would first like to thank my literary mentor and now good friend, **RAYMOND AARON**, for guiding me in the process of writing a book. It is because of his wisdom and high energy that I was able to get my book done so quickly. His mentorship and teachings have allowed me to partner and work closely in helping others achieve their lifelong goals. I'm blessed to have been introduced to you in that you have allowed me to reach out, connect, and work with others all across the world.

I am forever grateful in receiving the gift of having two angels in my life: my absolutely amazing daughters, **BIANCA LABOSSIERE** and **EVA LABOSSIERE**. You are both the breath of my soul. You exude such pride and respect, and bring about utopic happiness to me and every person who is blessed to be around you both. I deeply appreciate the hours you both spend in mastering gymnastics, the importance you place with your education, as well as exposing yourself in learning different skills, such as playing musical instruments and singing. I will forever be your blessed, loving, and proud dad.

I would like to thank my mom, **SUZANNE LABOSSIERE (and my late dad, ROLAND LABOSSIERE)** for raising me to be the person who I am today. I would not have been able to achieve all of my successes if not for the infinite love, admiration, patience, support, and guidance that you have always provided me, and continue to do so. In watching my parents act, and unconditionally devote their time in helping others, I learned the immense value and impact this brings about to others. I love you

Transform the Coal in your Soul to Diamonds

guys so much and always will. You are the Oprah's of my life, and I am thoroughly blessed to have received you both as my parents.

A big thank you to my brothers, **BERNIE LABOSSIERE** and **CHUCK LABOSSIERE,** as well as my sister, **KIMBERLEY LABOSSIERE,** for being the loving and caring siblings I grew up with. Even though I moved afar to pursue personal opportunities, you have always been there, encouraging me, and being around for Mom and Dad at all times. I am blessed to have all of you in my life, and I am proud to be part of our family.

I am deeply grateful for my extended family, which includes my current brothers/sisters-in-law, **SHERRY LABOSSIERE** and **PAT ROCH**, as well as my ex-brothers/sisters-in-law, **DAVID DOUCET & JEANNE**, and my ex-fathers/mothers-in-law, **RENE DOUCET & MARIELLE PLOURDE.** I am thoroughly blessed for having had your loving impact, support, and laughter throughout these years. Thanks for always being present with a smile in good times and in bad times. I am blessed that you all contribute to the development of my nieces, **KELSEY, KRISTIN, ADELE, and VIOLETTE,** and my nephews, **NAULT** and **EVAN,** who are all amazing kids.

I'm grateful for **VALERIE DOUCET**, the mother of our two incredible girls, for her contributions, implication, love, and continued support towards our two girls. Parenting involves many different people, and I do appreciate her collaboration and her effort, to continuously ensure that the two amazing girls we received as gifts in our lives continue to progress in their development, so that they can achieve their deepest desires in their wonderful life.

Thank you to **JOELLE BEAUBIEN,** for coming into my life. I'm continuously thankful, every day, for how privileged I am to

Acknowledgements

be so spiritually connected with someone who is family oriented, unequivocally caring, and non-judgmental. Your serene calmness echoes loudly to those around you, and your uncanny ability of always being present as a pillar of strength and love is a model to the world. Your unbelievable maternal skills are a reflection and a testament on how well-raised your incredible kids are. I'm blessed to continue this lifelong journey together with you, and I'm thankful for our reciprocal connection to the core.

A big heartfelt thank you, appreciation, and utmost gratitude goes out to some of my lifelong friends— **PATRICK PELCHAT, KARL CASTONGUAY, FRED JUNEAU, ETIENNE FALLU, ALEXANDRE CHARETTE, PATRICK GROLEAU, ERIC JENKINS, MATHIEU FLEURY and MICHEL TREMBLAY**— whom I consider family, since our ice hockey playing days at Concordia University, and our *never miss,* annual fishing trip! Gentlemen, I am immensely grateful. You are extraordinary friends. The laughter, teasing, and experiences we have had together throughout the past 20 years is merely a start to the wonderful years facing us. Not only am I grateful for your friendship, I am also thankful that you all have amazing wives too: **NATACHA, STEPHANIE, MELANIE, NATHALIE, ANICK, JULIE, NATHALIE, SUSKA, and JOSEE**. We know you are the backbone, and I am very appreciative and lucky that you, your husbands, and all the kids, are part of my life. Thank you for your generosity and support, through thick and thin.

For my post ice hockey career, kudos of appreciation goes out to the crew that has allowed me to play hockey with them every week in the winter, as well as to the other crew who joins us, along with some NHLers, once in a while during the summer months. I am deeply appreciative of everyone who joins us, and believe me, these individuals are all top notch people, and it's absolutely impressive. Thank you, as well, to **FRANCOIS**

Transform the Coal in your Soul to Diamonds

BLONDIN and **DAVID EILEY,** for organizing these sessions, year after year.

A special shout out goes to my friend, **LISA JANSSEN,** as she always believed in my talent. I am extremely grateful to have met you, and for all of our discussions over the years. It is because of you that I was able to take the appropriate steps in publishing my book. Over the years, my knowledge of wealth and experiences were stored within, and because of you, they are now offered to the world. I am so grateful, as these ideas are now in print for others to read and partner with me throughout our journeys together. Thank you so much for being the kindling to igniting the fire within me, in order to allow this book, and all the bonuses and information at my website, www.LeadershipKing.com, to be exposed to everyone around the world!

A word of gratitude to my medical team! I say this because I am so very fortunate to have some phenomenal and talented experts in their field, who help me proactively take care of my health and wellbeing, so that my body, mind, and soul can be aligned. My osteopath, **GENEVIEVE ARCAND, D.O.,** is not only very talented in her profession, she has an incredible holistic mindset, which I truly respect and connect with in full. Thank you to my reflexologist, **JOCELYNE BOULAIS,** and my massage therapist, **PATRICIA BOUCHARD,** for their incredible ability in keeping me and my muscles relaxed. To my family doctor, **DR. DENIS PROULX, M.D.,** for continuously ensuring that I am healthy so I can be there for my loved ones, and for his candid feedback when I am not!

It is a blessing to have so many incredible friendships, mentors, and examples of love in my life. These friendships are so near and dear to my heart, and all of you have contributed in helping shape me into who I am today. I am very proud and

Acknowledgements

humbled by our friendships. To my best men, **STEVEN MATRESKY, GREG HEFFERNAN, DONALD CHARBONNEAU, SHAWN FOSTER**, a virtual hug to all of you, as we all live in different areas across the world. Even though we don't see each other often in person, many thoughts of you guys, and my gratitude for our friendship, pass through my mind, and they mean so much.

To my buddy, **SYLVAIN COTE,** for embarking with me on different projects throughout the past many years. I appreciate that you were there during the good times, like you were there during some of the unfortunate, bad times. At the end of the day, I can say that at least in all of those situations, we always acted in a very dignified, ethical, and honest fashion, and worked to always find the best solutions as much as possible for everyone involved. Thanks for your courage, honesty, and friendship throughout all of those times.

A shout out to **SHAUN HEBERT, CONNOR STE-MARIE, and DAVE "Hurricane Category Forde" FORDE,** for making sure our annual, once-a-year golf retreat occurs, regardless of where we are in life. Shaun, a big thanks for our discussions, and for the wonderful memories we create every time we get together, and I look forward to more, for many years, bud! Connor, thanks for showing us that even young guys are cool! Dave, a huge appreciation for our friendship and for one that has grown over the many last years into us being soul brothers in regards to our deep, passionate care for other people. I am deeply honoured, and cherish all that each of you guys bring; so, thank you.

Throughout my professional career, I have been exposed to an incredible wealth of talented individuals, who I have had the privilege and honour to learn from. Whether or not they hold position titles of the highest ranking position, such as CEO, all have been in correspondence with me during my tenure, at some point. I am thankful to **BRENT SAUNDERS, WILLIAM (BILL) MEURY, MARC PRINCEN, MAURO NADDEO, ED GUDAITIS, CATHERINE BISSETT, and JONATHAN WONG,** for teaching me that taking bold actions in a transparent fashion is a characteristic of a leadership king. To **CLARE BLAKEY, RICHARD LAWFORT, and PAULA KELLY,** from International, for their warm and caring approach of immediately including me when I had transferred into my Senior Sales Trainer role. Your passion and kindness are truly appreciated; so, thank you, so very much.

Other people who I have worked directly under, on numerous projects, are the likes of Vice Presidents, such as **BRUNO MADER**; business unit directors, like **JOHN STEWART, ANDY ZYLAK, and GAVIN DAMSTRA**; marketing manager, **ENZA CIGNARELLA**; managers, like **PHILIPPE VALOIS, MARTINE RANGER, MARTHA BRIDGES, MARC ROBITAILLE, LAURA D'ANTICO, and FRANCOIS LE MOUEL;** as well as others whom I collaborated with on many others projects. My appreciation goes very deep in that you have allowed me to create solutions for both physicians and patients. You've helped me fully engrain my core belief in wanting to help others achieve their ultimate goals and desires in life. All of our collaboration throughout the years has helped me gain experience in getting my book published, and exercising some of my ideas.

For over 15 years, I was absolutely awestruck, and privileged to have had the opportunity to work with the most talented physicians in different areas of medicine. There are so many doctors, nurses, secretaries, other pharmaceutical employees, etc. (you know who you are), who know the impact that they had on me and how they have helped mold me into the person I am so grateful to be today. I would love to list them all, if I could list the thousands of these amazing and talented

Acknowledgements

people. Believe me, I recognize each and every one of you, and if you are reading my book, and you know me, you know you have had an impact at some level.

I wanted to extend an immense feeling of gratitude to the following people who have made an incredible impact in my life, even though I haven't met them. Thank you to **OPRAH WINFREY, ELON MUSK, RICHARD BRANSON, JEFF BEZOS, MARK ZUCKERBERG, MARK CUBAN, DALAI LAMA, WARREN BUFFET, QUEEN ELIZABETH, BILL & MELINDA GATES, ANTHONY ROBBINS, JACK CANFIELD, BRIAN TRACY, and STEPHEN COVEY,** for your teachings and spirituality, in order to make this world a better place. Although it would be an absolute blessing to meet with you, I wanted express my gratitude for your contributions you have made, and continue to do so, to the lives of others. Thank you for your leadership and vision, and I hope with what I learned from all of you, I can continue to help others in their individual journey, and help them achieve their goals.

For anyone else who has crossed my path, such as friends, acquaintances, other family, colleagues, etc., please take credit in that you have had an impact on me in one way or another; and for that, I am extremely thankful and humbled. You are all important to me, and I am truly appreciative of our friendships and relationships.

If we have not yet met, I would thoroughly enjoy having the opportunity to do so. Perhaps you have participated at some of my presentations, seen my work, viewed or heard videos, or maybe even read some articles. Whatever the case may be, I am extending my hand out to you in hopes of being able to meet you. You have purchased my book and are reading it to improve your current situation, and that sends a tsunami of warmth and happiness! Thank you in advance and I look forward to hearing

Transform the Coal in your Soul to Diamonds

from you. Since I am always on the move, please feel free to reach me anytime at www.LeadershipKing.com and I will make sure someone involved in my team responds to you. Thank you!

Chapter 1

How Old is Your Coal?

"It's not as though we can keep burning coal in our power plants. Coal is a finite resource, too. We must find alternatives, and it's a better idea to find alternatives soon, than to wait until we run out of coal..." – Elon Musk

What Fuel Are You Using?

You may be asking yourself, "What does that mean?" Is it what type of gas you are putting in your car? What you ate this morning? The thoughts that you are thinking? What?

The answer is, all of the above. Think about it.

You have the option to choose in life exactly what type of fuel you want to consume. When you pull up at a gas station, you have the option to put whatever kind of octane fuel into your car. You may have never thought any more about it than simply putting in the cheapest octane fuel possible. For breakfast, you may have been in a rush and decided to stop at the nearest drive-thru to pick up anything to curb your hunger, without thinking about what you are eating. You may be thinking about so many things, and not paying attention as to what *kind* of thoughts you are thinking about.

Transform the Coal in your Soul to Diamonds

These are only a couple of examples in order to make a couple of points. You see, you have the ability to control and decide what kind of fuel you want to use. If you had a high performance sports car, would you feed the engine with the cheapest octane fuel? Definitely not. The way those engines are built, they would cough and choke on trying to digest that fuel, and would want to immediately spit out what it consumed because it won't function at its highest efficiency.

Do you think that high calibre professional athletes consume non-nutritious food, multiple times a day? Not the most elite. The top athletes fuel their body by ingesting the highest quality of food they need, at their specific time in their training program, in order to achieve the highest of results or to take them to the next level.

What about your thoughts? Are you constantly thinking negative thoughts? Complaining? Gossiping? Or, do you exude positive thoughts? Are you achieving what you so much desire and deserve in life?

It's amazing when you take a moment and really think about what kind of fuel you are using. You may not have a high performance vehicle, or you may not be an elite athlete, and that's OK. It's not about that. It's about YOU. This book is going to bring you through a process of being conscious of what you are doing to yourself at different levels, and how can you transform yourself to being the most efficient YOU that YOU want to be. The only person that can decide this and take action is you. Nobody else. You will right away start to think of so many things that you never thought of before. You are where you currently are because you have settled and accepted that. You may not want to think or believe that, but it's the truth. The salary that you have accepted is a result of you accepting that amount as your perceived value. It's not that it's wrong; it just is. It's where you are at today. Just ask yourself the question as to why others, doing the exact same thing as you, may be making 2–3 times more. Are they better than you? Probably not.

Everyone has coal in their soul, which they have been using for so many years that they continuously keep polluting their soul unconsciously, and the results of doing that continuously add to this.

I have good news for you. Actually, great news for you! I am so, so, so excited for you! You are going to read this book in its entirety, as quickly as possible, and will take action to replace your own personal fuel energy source. You will understand and undergo a personal transformation. You may need little, some, or a lot of guidance, and that's okay. You and I will be able to work together and find a solution. Exciting for you, isn't it??

You live in the greatest transformational era, and can already see or hear about so many transformations in this world. Take a look at what Elon Musk is doing. He has revolutionized the automobile industry with his efficient, high performance electric cars. He is revolutionizing the solar energy industry. He is creating high energy battery packs. The great news is that he has got all of this, and way more, in the past 15 years. It does not matter where you are in your life, what you are currently doing, and what has happened in the past. You are in control of your own evolution. You decide. Today. Be present in the present. From now on, you decide what fuel you are going to use in every situation!

Is Soul Coal a *Fossil Fuel*?

To understand this, you will need to know what a fossil fuel is. Basically, a fossil fuel is a fuel such as coal, oil, or natural gas, formed in the Earth from plant or animal remains. If you look

Transform the Coal in your Soul to Diamonds

at coal, for example, you will see that it is a black or dark brown rock, found mainly in underground deposits that can be used as a source of energy or fuel. If you have ever played with a piece of coal in your hands, you will know that your hands will be full of black residue as a consequence. If you smell the coal, you can almost feel the residue being caked within your lungs as you inhale. According to scientists, burning coal is a leading cause of smog, acid rain, and toxic air pollution.

So what is *soul coal* then? It is basically all the negative thoughts, disbeliefs, fear, and anything else that is stopping or polluting your soul, dreams, and desires. The more *soul coal* that you are burning or using as your primary energy source, the more you are using techniques, strategies, and mechanisms that go *against* what you really want! The other problem is that there are so many people who are trying to give you THEIR *soul coal*. You have probably heard other people tell you that "you can't do that;" "you're no good;" "you don't deserve that;" "you'll never be able to achieve your dreams;" and you, unfortunately, start to believe it. They add so much of their *soul coal* on you that it suffocates and, basically, puts out the fire that burned within you. A fire needs 3 things to burn: heat, fuel, and oxygen. After reading my book, you will be able to understand how you will be able to refocus and reignite your inner fire. You will become the best scout at lighting inner fires within yourself, and keeping them bright and fully lit. You will strip away the *soul coal* you face, choose an alternate fuel, and heat your inner fuel to the highest temperature possible. Your changes will be remarkable.

After some of my lectures on stage, I have had people come up to me and share with me that, after applying some of my teachings; they began undergoing their own transformation. You are making that transformation too, by reading this book and becoming your own leadership king at whatever your strengths may be. You will also be able to get ample information from my

How Old is Your Coal?

website, www.LeadershipKing.com, and other exciting materials to add to your fire kit after you finish reading my book. I could give you To-Do lists, recipes, guides, and so on, to follow, right from the beginning, but I won't. Not yet. The most important thing this book will do is discuss your mindset and how you will take action to change it.

So, the answer to the question, "Is soul coal a fossil fuel?" is YES! Fossil means the remains or impression of a prehistoric organism preserved as a mold or cast in rock. It can also mean old and unchanging. That is the *old* you from the past. Out with the old you, and in with the new you!

So now, you are fully aware of a couple of things so far, and you just started! Be proud of yourself, and really start putting this into action. You've already learned that YOU decide what fuel you want to use in any situation. Be present and conscious of this at all times. You are already taking a leadership action by taking responsibility and assuming the choices you are now making, moving forward.

This takes me to the next learning that you have already made. You cannot change the past. It has already occurred. *Soul coal* is a fossil fuel. It serves no other purpose other than that it is old, and a source of energy that has been polluting your thoughts, desires, and dreams for way too long. Since you are now taking responsibility, and have the choice to make your own decisions, you will no longer use your own *soul coal,* or that from anyone else, as a source of energy, as of right now. Convert any negative remarks, thoughts or feelings into a positive, and tell yourself. Read it out loud, write down the positive words, feel the warmth of the positive fires you light within yourself. Your transformational evolution continues....

Stresses to Your Soul

Every stress, positive or negative, that happens to you, will be accommodated up to a certain tolerable degree. Beyond this capacity, the system breaks down. There are also different intensities of stresses that you will face throughout your life. Let's look at a couple of examples in order for you to fully understand this concept.

Imagine blowing up a balloon and tying it up. Let's also imagine that the balloon is perfectly round. When that happens, the pressure within the balloon is in a state of equilibrium. Basically, the pressure is evenly distributed within the balloon. Now, if you were to take your finger and push it into the balloon, what happens? The balloon will shift in such a way to relieve the stress that you are putting on the balloon with your finger. If you keep your finger there, the new equilibrium is set with a new pressure in the balloon. Therefore, the balloon has adjusted to the new stress that you applied to it. Yet stresses have different intensities. What if you were in that same position, with your finger pushing against the balloon, and someone else comes along with a pin and touches your balloon? Obviously, the balloon will pop! The system has, therefore, broken down. You know that stresses happen to you all the time, whether they are positive or negative. There are stresses that you create yourself (you pushing your finger into the balloon), and stresses created from others (the person who popped your balloon with a pin). The secret in this wonderful example is that you can control the stresses you bring upon yourself.

You can also control the intensity of these stresses. You may not think that you can control the stresses that others bring upon you; however, you can! You can decide proactively to put yourself in situations in order to minimize the outside stresses put on to you from others.

How Old is Your Coal?

Here's an example: Imagine you are working as a sales representative for company A, and you have a manager that is micromanaging your every move. You are constantly being told what to do, being given hundreds and hundreds of tasks every day, and they want you to give them everything *yesterday*, etc. They are constantly on your case, and this goes on day after day. Your heart rate is probably racing; maybe you are starting to sweat, and you feel helpless. You know and see that this is a stressful situation. Now, imagine you are still a sales representative but for company B, and you have a manager that believes in you and provides you with the tools in order to achieve success. Let's assume the results in both Company A and Company B are the same. The manager in Company B, however, allows you to create your own plan, and simply acts as a guide in order to help you achieve the desired results.

Which situation would you choose?

The vast majority would definitely choose company B as the ideal place to work. The external stresses from company A usually create a situation where the sales representative will go into a burnout, there will be a high turnover rate, or it will create an inharmonious environment, where *the balloon will eventually pop*. Therefore, if you are in a stressful situation (such as Company A), note that you can proactively choose another environment (such as Company B); where you are consciously able to choose an environment with less negative stress.

Here's another example: Did you ever notice that when you start a new workout program, there are always the same characteristics that come out? Maybe your muscles are sore, perhaps you were more tired because the cardio machine that you used was different than what you normally do, etc. In any regards, exercise is a positive stress to your body, and your body will adjust to this new stress until it reaches a new state of equilibrium. Once you reach this point, you will once again have to change your program and exercises, so that your muscles and body can once again adapt to the new positive stresses of the new program.

I'll share with you a personal story, and you will see how it relates to you. Back when I was a personal trainer, in my twenties, while I was playing college hockey, I can remember this one gentleman, named Ivan. Before he became one of my future clients, he approached me and stated that his routine wasn't giving him the results he needed or wanted. So, I asked him one question: "How long have you been doing your program?" He told me that he'd been doing the same thing for 2 years!! You see, his body had adjusted to his original routine, and it was, therefore, no longer a stress to his body. The result was obviously no gains. Ivan needed direction, and someone to guide him with a new program every 4 to 6 weeks in order to improve. As Ivan achieved top results, the strategies required to continuously have greater gains needed to become more and more specific.

How does the story relate to you? This same principle can be used in other aspects of your life. Ask yourself the following question, and be fully honest with your response.

Am I just going through the motions of everyday life, and letting life happen to me, OR am I really implementing everything I need to do in order to get everything I desire, by creating my own life?

If you answered honestly, you are probably simply letting life happen to you. As of now, though, be very excited! The reason is, now you know YOU control the stresses to your soul.

How Old is Your Coal?

Does Age Matter?

You may be asking yourself if it is too late. Or if you are too young or don't have enough experience. Does age really matter?

The answer is, absolutely not! You can be at any stage of your life, and still have dreams and desires that you want to achieve in life. You could be 12 years old and be told that you can't do this because you're too young. Yet if you look at the most recent winners of *America's Got Talent,* as examples, you have Grace VanderWaal, who you heard won as a talented musician, as well as Darci Lyne Farmer, who won as a ventriloquist and also for creating her own characters. Both achieved the highest of successes at around the age of 12 years old!! Imagine if both of them decided not to pursue their dream, simply because they thought or were told that they were too young. The world would have, unfortunately, never been exposed to their talent.

Have you ever heard of Ray Kroc? If not, next time you decide to go to McDonald's, you will no longer need to ask yourself who the founder was. Ray Kroc started that business at the ripe young age of 53 years old. Imagine if we didn't have the golden arches all across the world, all because Ray Kroc would have thought he was too old.

What about Doris Drucker? She started her business when she was 82, to manufacture a device she invented! In case you were wondering, her husband was the management guru, Peter Drucker.

So, it doesn't matter what age you are at, what your dreams or goals may be, and what you were trying to achieve in your life. Age does NOT matter. The only thing that matters is that

Transform the Coal in your Soul to Diamonds

you take action. You face certain laws in life. Take gravity, for example. In simplest terms, gravity is the force that attracts a body towards the center of the Earth. If you don't believe that gravity is a law, try jumping into a pool but staying in midair for 5 minutes (without the help of external support). Obviously, you will fall immediately into the pool.

Here's another example, where you will see and feel it may be applicable to you. It is in regards to Newton's first law of motion. Now your goal is to become a leadership king, and to polish yourself right up to the top. So, how does physics apply to you in today's world, when this law was first presented by Sir Isaac Newton in 1686? Basically, an object at rest stays at rest; and an object in motion stays in motion, with the same speed, and in the same direction, unless acted upon by an unbalanced force. How does such an old law apply to you and your goals? Take a look at the first part: an object at rest stays at rest. If you do nothing, nothing will happen. Since you're reading this book, this will not apply to you anymore, as you have already taken action on a few items so far, and will continue to take action throughout this book. You will also probably use, or need, some of the solutions you require to meet your needs, from some of the different components of my website, www.LeadershipKing.com (more on these multiple bonuses, later!).

If you look at the second part of Newton's first law—an object in motion stays in motion, with the same speed, in the same direction, unless acted upon by an unbalanced force—this will definitely be applicable to you. For example, you may have heard the saying that *insanity can be described as doing the same actions over and over, and expecting different results.* If you are doing the same things, day after day, and continuously wanting to have different results but you do not take any action in order to achieve that, your results will always be the same. That makes total sense. It is only when you take action in some form or fashion, and apply that strategy or action towards what you are looking to change, that you will see a change in direction. So, if you're not getting the results that you are looking for, change your actions.

Imagine you are a car salesman, and you are not getting the results that you anticipated. You have the same opening, same presentation, and attempts to close the same way, every single time. You may have a bit of success (especially if you have a motivated buyer), but odds are, you will not be as successful as you deserve to be. Why not change something you are currently doing? Why not find out what the potential buyer is specifically looking for? Or, why not ask and observe what one of your successful colleagues is doing? Do something different than what you are currently doing, and measure your success accordingly.

Since you are looking to *Transform the Coal in your Soul to Diamonds* you will need to create multiple actions, specific to you, to help you become a leadership king (for what you are looking to specifically change) and polish yourself right to the top.

Energy Efficiency

How efficient are you with your energy?

You probably realize that there are two components to this question. At one end, there is the aspect in regards to energy. At the other end, there is a concept of efficiency.

What kind of energy is your soul burning?

You previously learned, in a previous section, in regards to how *soul coal* is one type of energy that can be used as fuel to

Transform the Coal in your Soul to Diamonds

energize yourself. That being said, you also now know that the *soul coal* type of energy is no longer a source of energy for you, since you are already moving towards polishing yourself right up to the top. Therefore, the type of energy source you will now require will need to be one that will provide you with an unlimited amount of energy, regardless what your goals, dreams, and desires may be. You will require an energy source that also represents the cleanest, purest, and most renewable form that will generate the kind of energy required to make changes within yourself, to achieve the highest of successes. It is a special kind of energy that can only be created by you. Only you can create this type of energy for yourself. It is not a transferable energy, so no one else can use this. Only you. The value of this energy for you, however, is the maximum value you could possibly purchase. The absolute best thing about your new energy source is that it does not cost you anything to acquire. To plug yourself and your soul into this remarkable new energy source, and knowing exactly what you want.

At the end of this chapter, you will need to write down exactly what you want. We tend to focus on too many things at the same time, whereas in reality, we need to focus on the one big item that is the most important to us. Any actions we take need to be related on your continuous improvement in regards to that ultimate goal or dream of yours. By consciously understanding that concept, you will be eliminating all the inefficiencies around you, and streamlining your energy towards all the actions needed, in order to obtain your specific desire. Once you determine what that ultimate desire in your life is, you will have acquired your ultimate energy source needed, because this goal of yours is the most important goal you want to achieve.

If we look at the second component, which deals with efficiency, you will learn how to map out all the necessary aspects in order to take action to become the most efficient as possible, with all the different steps, in order to attain that goal. In other words, you will need to undergo different processes in order to fine-tune the actions required for you to attain your ultimate goal. And only you can choose to accept only the purest, highest octane fuel in your body and soul, in order to achieve this.

If you look at life, you will note that we are in a world where everything you do is based on becoming more aerodynamic fine-tuned. In other words, optimizing each thought, feeling, and action to such a degree where you reach that point of saturation, where you think you can no longer achieve more. Yet even once you get there, there are still methods to fine-tune even more, and reach beyond that barrier.

Let's look at an Olympic 100m sprinter such as Usain Bolt. He trained for 4 years, between every Olympics, in the hopes of taking hundredths of seconds off of his time, for a race that lasts under 10 seconds! He did this so well that he was able to be at the top of his form, winning Gold in three consecutive Olympic Games.

The last component to overcome, in order to create the highest Energy Efficiency for your body and soul, is that of barriers. What barriers have you set in your mind? What is limiting your Energy Efficiency? You will work on stripping these inefficiencies away.

Let's look at an example of barriers, and how, once they are overcome once, it seems like they are overcome quite easily afterwards. Who was the first person to break the 4-minute? The answer is, Sir Roger Bannister. After numerous setbacks, victories, and then setbacks, it was only on May 6th, 1954, in a time of 3 minutes and 59.4 seconds, where this barrier was broken. What happened after that? Only 46 days later, John

Transform the Coal in your Soul to Diamonds

Landy, of Australia, broke Sir Roger Bannister's record, with a time of 3 minutes and 57.9 seconds. So, what is the current world record for the fastest mile? It is an astounding 3 minutes and 43.13 seconds, set by Hicham El Guerrouj, of Morocco, on July 7th, 1999!

So, once you determine your ultimate, most important life goal, and create all the necessary strategies to fine-tune your goal to its highest efficiency, you will be well on your way to polishing yourself right up to the top.

Evolution = Evolve + Solution

To create an evolution within yourself, you need to find a solution that will allow you to evolve into where you want to go.

It's quite interesting when you hear people talk about their current situation. It's always surprising to see, after I have presented to a crowd of people, where solutions are presented, that people show that they want to evolve, yet most do not make the decision to take action in their own personal evolution. If you are not taking action on your own personal evolution, guess what...no one will.

The fact of the matter is that many of the solutions you are seeking, currently exist. You do not have to recreate everything in order to evolve. You just need to know where you are now, where you want to go, and apply all the most pertinent aspects to yourself and your situation, to maximize your personal evolution. You are living at a time where you have access to multiple solutions that allow you to evolve faster than in any other era this world has ever seen. I am continuously working on creating different solutions that will meet your needs. The only thing that you need is to take action when the opportunity arises for you.

How Old is Your Coal?

Let's look at an example to help you understand how this can relate to you. Imagine you are an apple tree, and your goal is to become the highest apple tree that there has ever been, producing the most apples 1 tree has ever produced. In order to do so, you will need to have the proper mix of sunshine, fertilizer, water, and protection from any other predators. In order to evolve towards your goal, you will continuously need to add the proper elements to your tree, at certain times, in order to continue to grow to your Highest Potential. If any of the items you require are not applied in helping you grow, your growth and evolution towards your ultimate goal will be reduced. Sometimes, there can be such a lack of care in applying the necessary aspects in feeding your tree the most optimal solutions, and your tree will start to wither, and perhaps even potentially die. You see, at all points, your tree is either growing or dying. There is no time where your tree is at a standstill. So, the next time you hear anyone say that they prefer the status quo; they are growing or dying, as there is no in between. It's quite logical, actually, when you think about it.

The best thing you can do is provide yourself with all the solutions possible to allow yourself to evolve fully towards your goal. It is so crucial that you know what you want, since everything else will align around that. I'm going to be very authentic with you. Most people do not like change. It involves work. In today's world, outside evolution is happening at lightning speed. If you decide not to evolve, you will be obsolete. You have seen many examples of this throughout the years—CDs, 8-Tracks, Walkman, Betamax—and the list goes on and on. So, in the end, this choice stems from you.

You should be very proud of yourself, actually! The action you are taking by continuing to read this book proves to me your willingness to create your evolution, and with the progression you have made so far, you will definitely want to keep reading

Transform the Coal in your Soul to Diamonds

into the next chapter. If you are important to yourself, continue reading, so as to learn everything you now can to make your tomorrow even better for yourself. You are going to learn how to convert your failures into victories!

Chapter 2

Failing Victories

"I had become so accustomed to succeeding that I no longer even remembered what it was like to fail." – Oprah Winfrey

Fail to Win

Whatever the experience, situation, or event that is influencing your life, you are the controller and you can modify the future outcome.

You know, it's very interesting that, in schools, the objective seems to centre mostly on NOT making mistakes, while in real life, we make mistakes all the time. Sometimes we make major mistakes, and those lead to failures. Therefore, it might seem like quite the Paradox to state that it is okay to fail, in order to win.

So how do these failures serve you?

The irony behind failures is that they actually help you turn them into victories. Failures allow you to understand what you do not want in your life. The experience gained in those situations allows you to change and modify your approach, and fine-tune yourself to become aligned with your ultimate desires. Basically, failures help strip away the inefficiencies of your success! This also allows you to gain experience—real life

Transform the Coal in your Soul to Diamonds

experience—to ensure a higher probability of continuous future victories.

Let's talk about an example: your first day on the job. Remember when you first walked in to wherever you work, for your first day on the job? Think about that time again. You most probably felt nervous, anxious, and somewhat fearful of the unknown. Yet you were the chosen person for this role. You got the job! The hiring manager had full confidence in hiring you since you had the skills to do the role. So you begin your day, ask some questions, and begin fulfilling your role in your new job. You go to punch out to finish the start of your new day, when your manager calls you into his office and shows you a big mistake that you just made.

What would you do?

There are multiple answers to this question. However, in order to grow, and gain experience, one must learn from their mistakes. Here's where I'm going to make a very big announcement. A big distinction.

It is okay to make mistakes and have failures.

It makes it who you are and shapes who you have become. The big distinction is how you ACT afterwards. You have the decision to throw yourself a pity party or step up to the plate, assume the mistake and/or failure, and use that as a learning experience in order to build off of it. By choosing the latter of the two, you will have already won.

Here's an interesting story of comparison in regards to a production line in the automotive industry. In company C, a major mistake occurred. The assembly line was halted, people were screaming and yelling everywhere, and the whole production came to a standstill. People began pointing the finger at each other, and anger and blame intensified to unbearable degrees. Everyone wanted to find out who made the mistake. No one cared about anything else except for wanting to find out who they could blame. In Company D, the production line had the same mistake happen. One of the managers immediately and quickly got a team together to correct it. They worked in harmony to ensure that the mistake itself was taken care of as efficiently as possible. No one was looking to point any fingers, and rather made the decision amongst themselves to take that failure and correct it. The production line never skipped a beat, and continued to produce accordingly. Obviously, the better solution, to the same problem, were the actions taken in company D.

If you ask all successful individuals, most will confess that they had major failures in their life as well. As a leadership king authority, even I had some. It makes you resilient and helps you to persevere towards what is important to you. Your approach and your mindset in understanding how to convert failures to victories, as quickly as possible, without focusing on blame and rather more on the solution, will allow you to reach, at some point, a state where you have so many successes, that you will not even remember what a failure looks like.

Where Do You Rank?

This seems like such a strange question. Yet it's actually very pertinent in helping you metamorphose to what you want or who you want to be. Maybe you would have responded by stating the title of what you do for work. I know when I ask this question in seminars, the response I usually get is one in relation to their work, since they usually associate their work to their identity. I usually find this answer quite interesting, actually. If you thought or answered the same way, does that mean that your work determines who you are as a person? I asked a question

Transform the Coal in your Soul to Diamonds

because if it was flipped around, would you be doing the work that you are currently doing? Probably not.

The reason is, if you were centered with your true desires, you would be doing exactly what is necessary in order to achieve them. If your answer is different than the title of your work, then you know that you are probably not necessarily as aligned to what you really want to do as you may have once thought you were.

The great news around this is that you are taking action right now, and changing your mindset as you continue reading. As this happens, your true, everyday actions will be more and more aligned, and true to your key values, identity, and sense of meaning. That is exciting!

You may have also answered in such a way where you have a ranking or certain status in a hierarchy. In those situations, you are usually forced to follow orders in a hierarchical fashion. Maybe you are in the Navy, or Armed Forces, or are a professor in a European country. Let's use the Armed Forces as an example. Even though you may feel very strong against the orders that are given, you must abide by those predetermined rules, and execute that order. Imagine being in a situation where you are asked to execute the orders, but deep down, you disagree with the orders. What do you do? That is a question that only you will be able to answer, as it depends on your deep core values. Note that you make the decision to accept any role or not.

Another way of looking at where you rank is whether you are playing to win or simply protecting the lead. Let me explain. Imagine you are a professional golfer. You are four strokes ahead of the next player, and you have 9 holes left. You may choose to play to win, where you continue to be aggressive and attack the green. Or, you decide that you have enough of a lead, and try to play conservatively in order to protect your lead. Both are okay. It really depends on what you decide to do and how comfortable you are with your strategy. You may play to win and, as a result of your aggressive play, you may extend your lead tremendously, or be penalized by certain hazards, due to your aggressive play. If you choose to protect your lead, your decision may allow others to catch up to you, or it may be the proper action you need to take in order to win the tournament. So, as you can see, there are different strategies or solutions that you may choose from. You must choose the best one that needs your inner soul criteria.

You can also see where you rank yourself in regards to the spiritual universe vs. one in the physical universe. In the spiritual universe, there is no ranking of where you are. Basically, you're focusing on your own personal life mission goal, and everything around that. There is no better or worse, top or bottom, number one or number two, etc. It just simply has to do with what you deem is the most important. It is not a competition, as it centers more on your Center. A great example of a company that acts in this fashion is Apple. They focus on what Apple can do, who they can serve, and how they can help. They are not concerned whatsoever about what the competition is doing—for them, it's about what they're doing.

What about you?

This serves as a great transfer into the next topic. Like Apple, you will need to strip down to the core.

Strip Down to the Core

Stripping down to the core is literally taking away all the barriers and myths that have been limiting you and your soul from achieving success in bringing you closer to your life mission.

There are two different kinds of paradigms that you will need to be aware of. One is internal and the other is external.

Internal stripping down to the Core literally means you having to change and reprogram your internal mindset. The first, and most absolutely important step, in order for you to do so, is attracting all the positive thoughts surrounding what you have determined is your ultimate life goal, from previous chapters. Once you attract these positive thoughts, you will need to generate ideas around your thoughts. From that, you will need to feel, see, hear, taste, and smell everything surrounding those ideas. Your emotions to those ideas have to be so strongly ingrained that you will do anything required in order to fulfill them. Once you complete that process, you will then be able to take action—take action in the direction of the flow of energy. It is not the time to be a salmon and swim against the current. By plugging yourself in the same direction as the energy flow, results will follow.

When one looks at the external paradigm, you will note that this is what others try to inflict on you. With your new internal strength, you will easily be able to tell who is trying to pollute you with their negativity. It is important to note that you are not there to try to change their actions. That baggage belongs to them. Most of the time, individuals who are not looking to change, won't. Therefore, you need to strip away the external negativity from your life. This may include letting go of certain people. For example, if you can think of someone who is always complaining, gossiping, and simply not enjoying life, then this is an example of an external paradigm that you need to strip away from your core. Basically, you need to strip down to only using the most functional components required to operate the purest of you. From that, you will continuously add other external components, and build your internal machine to the highest of levels.

I previously used an example of the Jamaican sprinter, Usain Bolt. Now, I'm going to refer to his coach, Glen Mills, so I can share how this will also have an effect for you as well. Coach Mills does NOT have one single athletic medal to his name. He does, however, have an incredible understanding of anatomy, agility, coordination, talent identification, and biomechanics. A lot of people forget that at 17 years old, Usain Bolt had a disappointing loss in the 200m heats at the 2004 Athens Olympic Games. It was after these games that Usain Bolt approached Coach Mills. Mills was aware of Usain Bolt's natural ability but also aware of his poor technique, which caused multiple hamstring injuries for Usain Bolt, prior to working with Coach Mills. Glen Mills had a two-year plan of pulling apart the sprinters technique, painstakingly breaking Bolt's bad habits, and then reassembling it all to create Usain Bolt in becoming today's world record man form. This process was a repetitive and challenging process, often requiring hours of video analysis to help correct the minutiae of both the individual and the race stages.

As a coach, Mills provided Usain Bolt with the necessary fine-tuning required by taking him in; hence, Usain became the leadership king in sprinting. Coach Mills is an example of a true technician, with a remarkable attention to detail, intricacies of race phases, technique, and execution, which he balanced with a developing of his athletes' psychological prowess, by integrating motivational work into their daily routines. So, even the most elite athlete in the world required guidance to help him strip down to the core, and then be built precisely and as planned, in meeting the desired outcomes of Usain Bolt.

This example relates specifically to you as well; anyone who's looking for change will need a coach. Even coaches have coaches! So, if you don't succeed at first, then try what the coach suggested to you the first time. Now you know where you stand, and understand that you will need a coach to help you achieve your personal goals.

Name Your Competition

How competitive are you? It's a question where you need to be honest with yourself in regards to your answer. Do you need to compete against others in order to display or conquer your superiority against them? Or, are you the type of person that simply needs to compete against yourself? Let's look at each situation differently.

When you compete against yourself, you decide to what level you want to play the game. In other words, it is linked more towards the goals and desires you personally have set for yourself that you want to achieve. The rules of the game are infinite. They never end. Therefore, there is no time that one must follow, except for the one that they have set themselves. The rules of the game are private and individualized to your paradigm. You are the referee, participant, and owner of the very important game you are playing.

On the other hand, if you really need to compete against others to fulfill the satisfaction of beating someone, then you prefer a situation that is more finite, where are you are exposed to pre-set conditions, and are outlined by rules that everyone, who is playing, is aware of and needs to follow. You can see ample examples of this with any sporting event, sales team promotion, etc. Most of the time, people view the situations as having winners and losers. The importance in all of this is you.

Failing Victories

What is important to you?

Whether you play in your own game or in a game set by others, you still need to fulfill the objectives set for you.

I will share a story with you. I have worked for over 15 years in the pharmaceutical industry, holding numerous positions in sales, marketing, and training. The culture of the companies I worked for was extremely important in that it determined if I was playing a game against myself (quotas) or against my peers (ranking system). When I worked for the companies that allowed me to compete against my own quotas, there was tremendous harmony and sharing of information between colleagues since we were all competing against our own numbers. Sales grew, the company had tremendous success, and the motivation amongst the sales team was high. Retention of employees was never an issue.

On the flip side, the company that instilled a ranking system created an environment of internal competition amongst colleagues. There was a lack of sharing of information since most wanted to be ranked higher than their colleagues, in order to earn higher bonuses. The morale was very stressful, there was a high turnover rate, and it produced an environment where rather than allow the company to grow harmoniously, there was internal conflict within the organization at all times. This happens all the time.

The important aspect here is that you need to decide what the playing rules are, and in which league you want to play in since you have the choice to do so. You also decide how big of a game you want to play. Are you content in participating in a league that is highly structured: an entrepreneurial league, non-profit league, and so on? You should start seeing clarity in that the decision you make should always come back to what your ultimate goals and desires are. It needs to match and be in harmony, or you will not perform to your highest abilities.

Take a look at the differences between Apple and Microsoft, and how they named their competition. Apple has always been trying to find solutions on how to continuously help students to learn, help teachers to teach, and integrate a platform (apps) in which the general public could access and produce solutions for others. They continuously work on allowing the masses to contribute to everyone. Microsoft produced software and an operating system that pretty well monopolized the market over the years. There were years where the software you would purchase had Internet Explorer already included as part of the software. Microsoft plays in a completely different set of rules in order to remain the dominant player, and did so for many years. I do not want you to misinterpret that either Microsoft or Apple's way of doing business is better than the other. It is just to show the differences in business philosophy between both of them. Wonderful initiatives created by both companies allowed the evolution of mankind. To go even further, Microsoft's success allowed Bill Gates to create the Bill & Melinda Gates Foundation, which is a remarkable foundation looking to create equality, regardless of people's lives, since everyone has dreams.

Emotional Training

How emotional are you?

Are you the type of person that looks at every situation from a rational point of view, and simply observes the situation objectively, without emotion, or are you known to be very emotional, and react to situations by wearing your emotions on your sleeve.

Think about that for a second. The reason I am asking you is so that you become self-aware of how you currently are. There's always a range between both, just as there is a range between street smarts and book smarts. If you are book smart, you understand the theory, and are very intelligent by providing answers from a theoretical point of view. If you are street smart, you may not know the theoretical answers; however, you find a solution to the actual situation at hand.

I named this section *emotional training* since it will be important for you to understand the range between logic and emotion, to unconsciously begin to train yourself emotionally. Let me explain. To obtain your deepest desires, you have already learned how this needs to be determined in full clarity: plan with many different strategies in order to help you achieve that ultimate desire, continuously fine-tuning along the way, with failures and victories, to help polish you right to the top. That is the logical solution plan. It will be the emotional connection that runs so deep within you that you have no other choice but to act, and to overcome the inertia that is holding you back. You will become so passionate and so willing to do everything in your power in order to achieve your desires, that those feelings and emotions will undergo an emotional training workout. Just like you may go to the gym to work on your body, or to the library to work on your mind, you will need to work on your emotions, and undergo emotional training to achieve your personal desires. A very important part of this training is in regards to emotional intelligence. You may be asking yourself what that means. If you don't know, that's okay, as you and I are here together on this journey to help transform your life.

Emotional intelligence is basically being able to recognize your own emotions, as well as those of other people. It's being able to filter the different feelings that are there, from your point

Transform the Coal in your Soul to Diamonds

of view, and from the other person's point of view, and being able to identify them appropriately. There are usually multiple components involved with emotional intelligence. A strong sense of self-awareness is important for you to understand. In other words, you will need to learn to be aware of what you are feeling in different situations, as well as what others around you are feeling. Motivation is also a component of emotional intelligence: what motivates you specifically, and understanding what motivates other people as well. Empathy is basically understanding, at a deep level, what the other person is currently experiencing, yet you do not get emotionally drawn in yourself. Social skills are another area for you to investigate, as it's becoming more important, especially in today's technologically connected world. Technology has transformed how we communicate with others, and the social skills paradigm has changed. You need to learn how to manage these relationships in order to help move people in the desired direction. One of the last components that will be important for you during your emotional training, in regards to emotional intelligence, is self-regulation. Self-regulation basically involves controlling or having the ability to redirect ones disruptive emotions and/or impulses, and adopting changing conditions.

Imagine you are at the gym. You are about to start your new program. You have hired a personal trainer whose role is to take you through a program that is specifically designed for you and your needs, at that specific moment in time. Imagine you have some sort of physical injury. Your personal trainer will need to adapt your program in order to ensure you are motivated towards your goals, and ensure, through communication, that you are aware of your strengths and weaknesses. Your personal trainer, or coach, will need to be empathetic and understand what you are going through emotionally, and what your goals and desires are, to help guide you in the proper path. Moving forward, today, you now know that emotional training will be necessary for you to acquire as part of your transformational toolbox.

Every Session Counts

Every experience that happens to you or around you, whether it is positive, neutral, or negative, will have an effect on you, whether you like it or not. Your experience can either be conscious or subconscious.

Regardless, the fact of the matter is that every situation will mold and shape you into becoming who you are at this present moment in time. The result? At some level, you realize that these events, in a certain way, are part of your world, and that they will affect you.

So every session counts.

The decisions you make are either adding towards your goal, or they are taking away from your goal. In order to achieve and go where you want to go, a conscious effort regarding all actions towards that goal will need to be magnified. You are faced with two kinds of actions: effective action and inspired action.

Effective actions are everything that you have outlined that requires focused effort. It's an effort where action-oriented decisions are made, which specifically help you move towards your desired goal. As we have been doing throughout this book, it is stripping away the inefficiencies of the time-wasters that are trying to take focused effort away from you. Imagine if you didn't have all of those distractions! You need to realize that effective action is specific to helping you act towards your goal. It is not just going through the motions and keeping yourself busy. Rather, it is highly specific.

Transform the Coal in your Soul to Diamonds

The other kind of action is *inspired action*. This feels more like fun rather than work. It is action that excites you to your deepest core, and it has nothing to do with winning or competition. I like to call these heart actions. The important part for you is just to realize that every session counts. In every decision you make, you choose what affects your outcome. You must also realize, acknowledge, and take responsibility to accept the consequences that come along with every choice. Remember that the chapter is entitled *failing victories*. There will be occasions where you will make decisions that will not be aligned with your deepest desires. As a leadership king, I am empathetic with that, as it is not logical to say that it will not happen. The difference is that you will need to hold yourself accountable for all the actions and decisions you make. All actions either bring you closer or take you further away from your goal. Sometimes you fail; sometimes there are victories. You want to ensure that the majority of your actions count and are directed towards victories. The more your actions are aligned with what you really, really want, the more victories you will experience.

Imagine you are on a cruise ship, and you see an iceberg way ahead of you and in your trajectory. In order to avoid the iceberg, you will make multiple decisions and take action at numerous levels (steering, speed, mapping of time, etc.). You will also do this ahead of time, and ensure that all the different actions you have taken count towards the common goal (to avoid the iceberg). Your cruise ship is so large that you are required to make every one of those little actions count, for the good of the common goal. This is the same thing that you will be applying, moving forward, to help you *Transform the Coal in your Soul to Diamonds*. You have already learned so much so far, and you have just begun! The next chapter is so exciting, as you will see the value of where you can, and will, end up.

Failing Victories

Keep reading so that you can hear, see, and feel what the value of your uniqueness is worth!

Chapter 3

Value of Soul Diamonds

"Price is what you pay. Value is what you get." – Warren Buffett

Scarcity Creates Highest Value

Did you ever notice that items in the world, which are the scarcest, usually have the highest exponential value?

This goes for everything. Economists like to call this the law of supply and demand. Supply represents how much the market can offer. In other words, the quantity supplied refers to the amount of a certain good producers are willing to supply when receiving a certain price for it. Demand, on the other hand, refers to how much of a product or service is desired by buyers. Therefore, if there is very little supply of a certain item, but there are millions and millions of people who want to acquire it, the value, or price of that limited supply, will be extremely high. After reading this book and following through by taking action for yourself, you will be in high demand.

Let's look at a couple of examples. You may see or read about certain artwork collectors purchasing very rare, highly sought-after artwork, for millions of dollars. Have you ever seen Picasso's painting: *Nude, Green Leaves and bust?* Did you know that he actually created it in one day? It sold for 106.5 million dollars! If you are a baseball card collector, you will know

Transform the Coal in your Soul to Diamonds

that the Honus Wagner baseball card is the world's most precious baseball card: one was recently purchased for over 3 million dollars. If you like to drink wine, you will have ample examples of different rare bottles of wine that are worth millions of dollars. Would you pay $232,692 to purchase one bottle of Chateau Lafite Rothschild, from 1869? Well, someone did. Not only did they buy one bottle, they purchased 3! That's approximately $29,000 per glass!

So, why am I using these as examples?

Scarcity creates the highest value, when everyone wants you. You need to understand the concept that being rare, unique, and the expert in your field, for what you desire, will position you and brand you as having the highest value. In other words, the scarcity of what you offer, as a person to your own goals, as well as to how that can help others, will make you infinitely valuable. Transforming the coal in your soul to diamonds is precisely that. The value of your *soul diamonds* is incredibly valuable due to its scarcity. There is only one you. You are unique and rare, and will polish yourself right to the top. This is exactly what happened to me in becoming an authority as the *Leadership King*. You will be so much in demand because of your uniqueness and value, that your options will be limitless.

It is incredible to note the different values that are placed on what most people consider as the most precious mineral in the world: the diamond. It is also interesting to note that both the Sancy diamond and the Koh-I-Noor diamond are non-estimated, and are priceless in terms of value. Take the action you need, and make your soul diamonds non-estimated, and priceless as well!

Create your own scarcity, and the demand for you, as a consequence, will have no boundaries. In other words, understand that all the actions you partake into polishing yourself to your specific goals and aspirations you have set for yourself, will develop the highest value for you, since you will be the utmost, optimal rarity.

As you transform yourself to this valuable stage, the contribution your value will provide to the world will be of the highest value possible. For that, you must congratulate yourself for taking action in doing so. For those around you, who unfortunately decide to do nothing, they will have decided to miss out on the opportunity of creating the highest value for themselves. The fact that you are continuing to read my book, and are continuing to alter your mindset, shows that you are well on your way to polishing your soul diamonds.

The Most Abrasive Mineral in the World

What are the first things you think about when somebody says the word, *diamond*? Do you think of the words, *shiny, beautiful, rare*, etc.? Most probably.

Do you ever think of the word, *abrasive*, when you think of diamond? Probably not.

The definition of abrasive is being able to polish, or being capable of polishing, a hard substance by rubbing or grinding. Basically, diamonds can be used to shape a workpiece. And that work piece is you. In order to shape yourself, you will need access to the most abrasive mineral in the world, that being of your own soul diamonds.

Diamonds are the hardest, naturally occurring mineral known in the world. In terms of hardness, it actually scores a 10 on the Mohs scale, which is the highest rating. Therefore, even though you have access to your soul diamonds, which are shiny,

Transform the Coal in your Soul to Diamonds

beautiful, rare, and more, you also have access to the most abrasive mineral in the world. Your soul diamonds are to be authentic, real, and true. You have no room for imitations in your soul.

The utility of this is in regards to you being resilient. Being resilient is basically being able to withstand or to recover quickly from difficult situations. You have faced difficult situations in your life. Everyone has, including myself.

Actually, I will share a personal story with you that I have rarely shared with anyone. There was a time, a couple years ago, where I underwent a separation from my wife of 19 years, a loss of my father whom I loved dearly, and a change of employment, as well as dealing with one of my businesses that was facing an extreme change of conditions, for the worse. All at the same time! For an outsider, they didn't necessarily see, feel, or experience what I was going through. Yet, internally, there were multiple tornadoes, occurring all at the same time, all in the same place. I had the choice of how to face these challenges. Being very grateful in having the choice of how to act and behave in each situation, I was able to overcome all of those conditions to the best of my abilities. The absolute best. Once I did that, there was nothing more I could do. Some were more difficult than others to overcome; however, applying the best strategies in each individual situation allowed me to grow towards becoming more resilient. In other words, I polished myself in every separate challenge, and became more resilient as a positive consequence.

Think about a recent challenge you faced.

What did you do? What actions did you take to overcome that challenge? How do you feel about overcoming the obstacle that was in your way? What were the thoughts you were saying to yourself in order to be encouraged in finding a solution?

Using your soul diamonds to retool your inner spirit, by learning from the failures you have had in your life, makes you more and more resilient to failure. As you become more resilient, you will note that any obstacle or challenge you may be facing will become smaller or insignificant.

You just learned that soul diamonds are the most abrasive minerals in the world. Unfortunately, there is also another definition of abrasive. This other meaning is the showing of little concern for the feelings of others. I wanted to share this other meaning with you because sometimes people will choose to be selfish instead. They have an ego, and all they want is to have everything for themselves, to the detriment of the feelings of other people. In other words, the value of their soul diamonds may create a perception of high value in their minds, yet in reality this value is worthless to others. Zero. I like to term these individuals as having *soul cubic zirconia*. Although it may resemble a diamond, it is NOT a diamond. Fake. Phony. Wannabes that imitate. As for you, be authentic, and harvest the true soul diamonds in your inner spirit.

To be a true leadership king, I know you will want to work with your own soul diamonds—the real you, working on the real mission as to why you are wanting so much to polish yourself to the top, in whatever you have decided, in previous chapters, to polish. The beauty of soul diamonds is that they come in all shapes, sizes, and colors. Every soul diamond is unique, and simply needs to be extracted. You will read more on this shortly.

Mine Your Soul

Have you ever heard of the Crater of Diamonds State Park that is located in Arkansas?

Transform the Coal in your Soul to Diamonds

If you haven't, it is the only diamond producing site in the world, where you and anyone else can actively search for diamonds.

There is one catch though...

The diamonds you find are yours to keep! People come from all over the world, and pay a price that ranges from $6–$10, in the hopes of mining some diamonds there.

The flip side of the story is that you have to realize that you actually have access to your own diamond mine—within yourself! So, you don't even have to look anywhere else. You may not know how many diamonds you have at this moment, which should be exciting to you, but you know that they are definitely there. You may not know what tools are required in order to mine your soul; however, you know that I am there to help find a solution. So, that's okay, for now. You will soon learn that, in order to extract the maximum value of yourself, you will need to know what you want and the steps on how to get that, and invest in the tools required, specific to you only, in order to mine your soul.

I'm going to share with you a very important concept. It is preferable that you *mine your soul* rather than have someone tell you *your soul is mine*. In this world, there are greedy miners out there looking to exploit the diamonds in your soul. They will utilize different tools and strategies with you in order for you to give them the right to mine your soul for those ever-precious, valuable soul diamonds. You have the choice to accept those conditions, or not. I am going to go out on a limb here to say that if you are reading this book, you are now allowing that to happen, right?

Value of Soul Diamonds

This book was designed specifically with the purpose for you to mine your own soul of its precious resources. It is time for you to stand up, take action, and mine your own soul, for the rewards that you truly deserve. It is time for you to tell others to *mine their own business, while you mine yours.*

Your time to mine starts today. It's all about the ABCs! People who are not **A**chieving, are not **B**elieving, because they're **C**heating! Take a look around you. In a short period of time, you will notice that someone you see is doing something that is harmful to their health. They may be smoking, eating a high-calorie, non-nutritious meal, or waiting behind a crowd of people in order to take the elevators rather than the stairs, to go up one flight of stairs. Perhaps there is a newspaper nearby. Open it to any page and you will see scandals, negativity, and disasters. Cheating. Misery. People are predictable, and so are their actions. The difference is that now you know you are the controller of your actions, and can thereby alter decisions with your choices. Here is where you decide consciously to change—for you.

Have you ever heard of Pareto's principle? Or the 80/20 rule? In simplest terms, it basically means that 80% of the effects come from 20% of the causes. In other words, if you were working in sales, it would mean that 80% of your sales comes from 20% of your clients. So, where would you concentrate your efforts? You bet! You would spend and nurture those 20% of clients. The richest 20% of the world's population controls 80% of the world's income. I am sure you can think of other examples quite easily.

How does this relate to you?

As you continue to invest in yourself, and mine your soul to extract your highest value, with all the necessary tools required, you will need to begin mining in the proper 20% area of your soul. This will allow you the highest probability of polishing yourself to the top, with the best results, as a reward of your efforts.

Sharp Defined Edges

Have you ever heard of the saying, *you are a diamond in the rough*? I actually believe this to be true with everyone, including yourself. You have certain strengths to offer, as well as dreams, desires, or goals that you want to achieve. It does not matter where you are currently, or what age you are at this moment. The most important part to realize is that your soul diamonds are all currently a little rough around the edges. For now. You just need to extract them from your soul, polish them, and cut them into sharp defined edges. Rather than having your dreams or goals being blurry, you are going to continue to read this book to ensure that they become crystal clear.

I shared with you, in an earlier chapter, in regards to obtaining specific tools that you will require, to work on *you*. One of these tools, metaphorically speaking, will have diamond tipped blades in order to create sharp defined edges within you. You'll be able to obtain more of that information upon completing this book and, afterwards, can refer directly to my website at www.LeadershipKing.com. You will learn, and have access to, information to help better your current situation. In other words, you become an expert gem cutter. The only exception is that the only gems that you will cut and polish will be your own, and no one else's. Therefore, even if you wanted to bring your gems to another gem cutter and have them work on your gemstones, sharp defined edges will always be rough and jagged. The only way to develop your crystal clear, highly precise edges is to do the work on yourself, yourself. To learn your new trade, it is absolutely imperative to acquire knowledge on how to do so for

Value of Soul Diamonds

yourself. Yes, everyone has a coach, expert, or mentor, and that is extremely important. Coaches have coaches. It is necessary for you to do so, too, in order to learn how to optimize and create the highest quality product for you.

Let me share with you a couple of examples.

Have you ever looked through a camera lens that was not in focus? What did you see? Obviously, the images where blurry and undefined. In other words, they were not sharp. Would you take pictures with your personal camera that was always blurry? Definitely not. The same goes for your personal goals. Your desires are attainable. You will need to take your camera lens, and zoom into your soul, and focus the desired image so that it has sharp defined edges.

Another example would be putting on somebody else's eyeglasses that are a strong prescription. You'll instantly see blurry, probably get a headache, and your eyes will start to water. Your soul has the same reaction when it is not aligned with your desires. Love yourself, and clarify the image for your soul. In terms of taking care of your eyes, you visit the optometrist, or ophthalmologist, to ensure that your vision is crystal clear. You will now need to make an appointment and visit *you*—your personal gem cutter—from now on, and cut your diamonds to fit perfectly within the diamond holders in yourself, like a diamond fits perfectly in a ring. You know that gem cutters work under high resolution, magnified lenses to ensure that their work is precise—so, focus on you!

You learned it is necessary to create sharp defined edges. You will need to know that it is important to realize that these sharp edges can cut deep. In other words, if you have sharp edges that you have never dealt with, these can continue to hurt you, or even others. I refer to this as your *scars of the soul*. A scar is a mark left by a healed wound. I'm very excited to inform you that your new sharp defined edges, which you create, will not create scars on your soul, or on anyone else's. It will heal yours, instead.

You will also now have a new edge to your personality. Basically, you will consciously know how to resist or reposition yourself, if there's something that irritates you. You will also no longer allow people to take advantage of you; if they try, the new sharply defined edges of your personality will be so sharp that they will not want to cut themselves on you. At that point, you will be your own master gem cutter.

Mirrored Prism

Do you know what a prism is? If not, take a look at Pink Floyd's cover for their album, *Dark Side of the Moon*. You will note that the prism is a transparent object, especially one that is triangular, with refracting surfaces at angles with each other, which separates white light into a spectrum of colors. If you think about it, it's like taking your soul diamonds and passing through your ultimate life goal or desire (white light), and reaping the different rewards (spectrum of colors) as a consequence!

The reason why I am referring to a mirrored prism is that the white light that you are emitting from your soul needs to be so exact to your desires, that before having it undergo transformation within your diamonds prism, it needs to hit the prism at a 90 degree angle and, therefore, reflect back to you. You will want to make sure that the reflection you will receive is exactly what you want to portray. If it isn't, you now know that certain tools and guidance will be required to ensure that it matches specifically what you are so passionate about, prior to showing this to the rest of the world.

Value of Soul Diamonds

Did you know that light changes speed as it moves through a prism? That is actually why there is a bending of the light as it undergoes this phenomenon. It's very interesting because, as you determine your ultimate life goal, there will be certain priorities (certain colors) that you will need to focus on first when these separate into different components (different colors), before focusing on other aspects (other colors). Do the first things first. You recently learned about this prioritization when you read about the 80/20 principle. Since color is the visible manifestation of the light's wavelength, the different colors of the rainbow will be separated accordingly. Focus on the right colors first. You will continue to learn how to do so as you and I move along together.

What about sound frequencies? Did you know that the human audible range is usually between 20 to 20,000 Hertz (Hz)? Why is this important to you? It is important for you to realize that you can hear sounds, or detect them, if they vibrate within those frequencies. As we age, we have a loss of sensitivity to higher frequencies. The interesting part in all of this is that there are animals that are able to hear frequencies that are smaller or greater than the audible frequencies that you can detect. For example, dolphins can hear frequencies up to 100,000 Hz, whereas some whales can hear sounds as low as 7 Hertz! That means that there are sound frequencies traveling through the air, water, and other material in which you may not be able to detect, whereas others will be able to. It simply proves the point that just because you can't hear them, it doesn't mean that they don't exist, because they do. This is important because what you think you are not projecting to others, you most likely are. Become a tuning fork. Create a personal frequency that vibrates in harmony with your inner thoughts and feelings, which will allow you to be in full tune with yourself.

Transform the Coal in your Soul to Diamonds

You will need to determine the brightest white light within your soul, to maximize the ultimate full reflection of colors as it passes through your soul diamond prism. Shadows will threaten this. You now know, however, that as you transform the coal in your soul to diamonds, you will search for that blinding light that will expose you, rather than the shadows that will dim you. At that point, your diamond prism will truly reflect your mirror image of your deepest desires—like Pink Floyd's famous song, *Shine on You Crazy Diamond*!

Unlimited Resource

Normally, you would think that resources would be limited. Your needs and wants may be unlimited, but most of the time, resources are limited.

So, how can you create unlimited resources?

The answer to that question is that you choose the renewable resource. As you've seen throughout this book, you choose the fuel you put within your soul, and you choose the outcome that is produced. All along that time line, you decide the steps necessary in order to create the most efficient resource to be used. That resource is unlimited, and you have infinite access to it. Having infinite access means that your dreams and desires will never fade away, never dim, and will always be a burning passion within your soul.

The fact that your soul diamonds have such high value, and unlimited potential, you will have to be aware of its power.

Let me share with you a famous fable in regards to the goose that lays golden eggs. One day, a farmer and his wife discovered that one of their geese was able to lay a pure golden egg. Like clockwork, this goose would lay one golden egg, every single

Value of Soul Diamonds

day. The farmer and his wife soon became very rich and wealthy as a result. Unfortunately, greed started to show its ugly face within their household. You see, the farmer was not satisfied with only having the goose lay one golden egg per day. So, he figured, why not kill the goose and open him up in order to collect all the golden eggs that would be within, and become richer faster. Well, if you know the story, you are aware that there were no golden eggs within the goose, and the farmer just ended up destroying the one thing that allowed him great wealth.

The moral of this story is that you have access to your own unlimited resources—your soul diamonds— which have infinite value for what they can produce. Like the goose that laid one golden egg per day, the process of your transformation in how to be a leadership king by polishing yourself right to the top, is one that involves consistent effort, desire, and the willingness to take action to do whatever is required, every single day, in order to cultivate the necessary rewards. Knowing the potential pitfalls ahead of time is important since you can choose actions that will always allow you to stay on the right course.

Think about all the different transformations that you have experienced throughout your lifetime so far. Through the use of water and turbines, electricity is being produced. Windmills and solar panels are converting wind and sun into energy. Recycling programs in the past 20 to 30 years have undergone major transformations, and reduced the amount of waste in our landfills. The list goes on and on. Many items in your external environments have undergone such transformations by utilizing strategies to create results from renewable and clean resources as much as possible.

The next great transformation to occur is happening right now. Yes, right now as we speak. This transformation is what is occurring inside of you. It is an internal transformation, and one

Transform the Coal in your Soul to Diamonds

that will revolutionize mankind. Mark my words; you will be a part of that metamorphosis. So, get ready! The next chapter will cover information on how to go about this. This is not a time to put the book down. Rather, you should be so excited on being part of this movement! So, do not skip a beat, and move right away to reading the next chapter. You will soon come to agree that your decision was well worth it.

Chapter 4

Where to Find a Leadership Polishing Kit

"A genuine leader is not a searcher for consensus but a molder of consensus." – Martin Luther King, Jr.

Polishing Soul Coal into Soul Diamonds

It is now time to polish your soul coal into diamonds. If you are still searching for the meaning of this metaphor, it is all about changing your internal mindset. It is knowing exactly what you want, and knowing precisely where to get what you need. The word, *polish*, is important to you because it basically shows you how to improve, refine, or add finishing touches. It is ensuring that there is a luster or soft glow, especially on all the reflective surfaces in your soul. You guessed right: your soul diamonds.

This book is all about transformational leadership. The first transformation occurs internally, followed by how this translates for you in the external environment, afterwards. Before I get into some of the important aspects regarding transformational leadership, which I will share with you very soon, I would like to compare this to a process that will be very clear for you to understand. That process is one in which how a butterfly comes to life.

The metamorphosis of a butterfly's life cycle undergoes four stages. The stages involve the egg, larva, pupa, and adult. Each stage is very important in order to move on to the next stage. It requires certain sequencing where the stages need to follow each other in that specific fashion. The order can't be changed. This holds true for you. You will need to follow a certain sequencing to maximize your transformational change. For instance, in the egg phase, the egg shape depends on the type of butterfly that laid the egg, and it is important that it is laid on the right kind of leaf. When the egg finally hatches— stage 2— butterfly larvae are actually what you would term as caterpillars. Their goal in this stage is to eat the leaves that they were born upon, and grow quickly. Once they have stopped growing, the pupa stage emerges. You would probably call this the cocoon stage. From the outside, you would probably think that the caterpillar within is simply resting. In reality, the caterpillar inside is rapidly changing. It is undergoing its metamorphosis. The last stage is one in which the adult emerges as a beautiful butterfly. Multiple components can occur at each stage, which will hinder the development of the butterfly's life cycle. This holds true for you as well, in regards to your transformation, which is why you and I will work closely to ensure your development reaches its maximum peak.

Everyone is at different stages of their development. Where you will start will be much different than where other people will be starting from, and that's totally normal. The speed of your development will also vary. You may need full handheld guidance, or you may simply need a little bit of direction. Regardless, you will always have access to a passenger, with a map beside you, to help you get to where you need to go.

Think of the following example. Imagine you are on the German Autobahn. This is the federal controlled highway system that is in place in Germany. Depending on which section you are driving in, which lane you have chosen, and what type of vehicle you are driving, will determine at what speed you are allowed to drive. Having you become a leadership king by polishing yourself right up to the top is basically providing you with a vehicle in which you can drive with no speed limits, and remain in full control. This will happen to you if you choose to take action. You are required to get in the car, put your key in the ignition, and take control of the vehicle. Once you do this, rather than bringing your car in for an interior and exterior cleaning, you will immediately bring yourself to a polishing garage, and learn how to polish your inner soul, and everything on your exterior as well.

Become a Chemist

Did you ever get that feeling, when you met someone, and something just clicked at a different level?

It's quite remarkable when it does occur, as the thoughts you are feeling are simply magnetic. You are thinking and feeling the same emotions as the other person, at multiple levels. Your heart rate is accelerated, and perhaps you're sweating a little bit; it might be the release of your human pheromones, the physical and mental appeal, or some other undetectable reason.

Remember when we spoke of the audible range? At this point, I'm going to describe this, and compare it to a dog whistle. When you blow a dog whistle, what do you hear? Nothing. It emits frequencies that are out of the range of the human audible frequency range, yet dogs respond. How can that be? How can these things occur without you being attuned to it? It seems like a reaction that occurs at multiple levels. Sound familiar? Go back and relive the feeling you had when it *clicked* with someone. The attraction, affinity, and avidity can be so powerful that this translates into an accelerated reaction. You can't explain it yet you feel it. The opposite is also true. You can probably quickly think of a time when you met someone, and you immediately knew you were both not compatible at certain levels. In chemistry, any action can be accelerated or slowed down with the effects of introducing an enzyme, which serves this role. Therefore, for anything you do in life, you can either accelerate or slow things down. You are the enzyme in all actions and reactions. You can either contribute to the situation or you can take away from the situation. Either way, you still make the decision.

For any kind of chemical reaction to occur, there must be a certain threshold that must be overcome. Being the chemist you are, let's look at another biological reaction example in order to fully understand. That example is the action potential of a simple muscle contraction. To keep this very simple for you to comprehend, your muscle will either contract or it won't. In other words, it needs to have enough certain chemicals transported to the muscle receptors, and for this to go over the minimum amount threshold required, in order for the muscle to fire (contract). All or none. If you don't have enough, there is no possible contraction. This is true with your dreams and desires. If you don't bring enough energy and necessary items forward, your dreams will not be put into action. Bring it.

Using this analogy as an example, in every situation you encounter in life, at a basic level, you either act or you don't. You may conjure up some thoughts or feelings about something, but this may not be enough for you to cross the necessary threshold needed for you to act on it.

So what are you doing about this?

You need to add the right chemical or enzymes to that specific situation in order to make it occur. Become a chemist. Be the creator of reactions within yourself. You need to add more chemical to the equation, as well as have the right enzymes to accelerate the reaction you are searching for, or looking to create. In other words, the goals or objectives that you have set for yourself need a step-by-step approach in order to attain them. You need a plan. A formula. A guide. As in any chemical reaction, you need to have the right formula in order to obtain the result you are attempting to achieve. I deliberately used the word, *attempt*, because you won't necessarily achieve the results you're looking for the first time you act on it. You will make mistakes. You will adjust. That's okay. There are many variables in any reaction, and sometimes you will not know what unknowns exist. There are always multiple tests done in every experiment to obtain the most desired output. Mentors are there to help you figure out why your chemical reaction is not working. Therefore, you must always remain a chemist of life, for life—your life.

Do you realize how many basic elements exist in chemistry at this moment?

There are approximately 118 elements in today's periodic table. These elements each have specific characteristics and attributes, different molecular weights, and difference valances. All of these differences are present for you to use when you are looking to create a chemical reaction. Just like some of these chemicals, some things are vital to our existence, and you will need to become a chemist of your soul. All thoughts, feelings, and actions you create, will dictate your outcomes accordingly. Become a master chemist of controlling your actions and reactions.

Open Up Your Own M.I.N.E.ing company

When you started reading this book, you probably did not think that I would tell you the next two things. First of all, you need to open up your own business. Secondly, your business needs to be very selfish at first. Now you are probably shaking your head, wondering why I would make such a bold statement. The answer is in the subtitle of this chapter, and that is to open up your own *M.I.N.E.ing* Company!

What does that mean? M.I.N.E. stands for My Interior Never Ends. So, yes, I am asking you to open up your own *My Interior Never Ends* company! My previous statements now make sense to you, don't they?

You are now in the business of personal entrepreneurship. Since your *My Interior Never Ends (M.I.N.E)* motto has now been opened, you will soon be offering a product, process, or service, for sale or hire. That creation will be you. You are the final product, process, or service that will contribute, through achieving your ultimate goals and desires, impactful positive contributions. Entrepreneurs, like you, often exhibit positive biases on how you see things. You are most likely to exploit the opportunity. Some of the exploitation resources that you will need, as you open up your *M.I.N.E.ing* Company, will be:

- Having a crystal clear *My Interior Never Ends* life mission
- Developing a specific plan to guide actions towards your life mission
- Providing leadership
- Taking responsibility for all successes and failures
- Hiring the proper consultants (i.e., coaches, mentors, etc.)
- Acquiring financial and material resources (i.e., educational courses towards the benefit of you)
- Taking calculated risks (innovation, continuous process improvement, etc.)

As you move forward, polish, and extract the beauty from within you, you'll note that everything has substance and acts differently in different situations. For example, think about what air is. You breathe air, but you don't see it. When you heat air, the particles get excited and move around quickly. The opposite occurs when the air is cold. When you apply force to air, you create wind. Propane is a gas that has no smell or color, yet it is still a substance. Actually, smell has to be added to propane in order for your senses to detect it. If you do not know what propane smells like, turn the knob to open the valve on a barbecue, without igniting it. How this relates to you is that you need to focus on the right substance when you open your own *M.I.N.Eing* Company.

The reason why your *My Interior Never Ends* Company will survive is perseverance. This means being tenacious, and doing something despite any difficulties or delays in achieving success. The sobering truth, and this may be hard for you to believe, is that 90% of start-ups fail. Only 10% succeed. You will now begin to understand why I have spent so much time, within the previous chapters, providing you with numerous, different concepts to fully understand, and why all your thoughts, feelings, and actions need to be fully aligned with you and your desires. If they are not, your success may be hindered. This book, and any other tools provided afterward, will help you avoid those pitfalls. Actually, there are certain statistics that exist as to why 10% of start-ups succeed, like you will as well, so choose perseverance.

One of these characteristics is that the product (you) is perfect for the market (your goal)—another thing you do to ensure that you do not ignore anything. You take into consideration all aspects, at all levels. Like the plant we spoke about in the previous chapter, your personal company (you) needs to grow, and as fast and as scalable as possible. You are living in an ever-connected world. Everything you need to do to transform yourself to where you want to go needs to stay ahead of the technology curve. Leverage this technical advantage.

Lastly, you will need to ensure that you have access to solutions (coaches, mentors, etc.) should you ever face any challenge in your transformational journey.

Become a Polishing Apprentice

In order for you to learn, let's face it, you will need to become a *polishing apprentice*. If you have children, you know they are who they are because of your influence on them. You are reading this book for that purpose. If you weren't, you would already be doing what you wanted to achieve in life. So, the first thing that's important is that you congratulate yourself for taking the initiative and the first step in your polishing apprenticeship, and that's reading this book in its entirety. You will probably even want to reread it to fully grasp all the information.

Some apprenticeships can be short if you can learn the trade relatively easy. Others can take years, or even a lifetime, for you to master the skills required. A good friend of mine was an apprentice for 4 years, as an Engineer, before he was able to get his own stamp! The most important skill, therefore, is that you are always open to learning, and that you continuously move forward. Big changes in your life are a result of all the little actions added together. Sometimes you will even experience a superimposed additive effect!

At this moment, you are gaining an understanding and learning more about the classroom theories—the book smarts components. This will be approximately 20% of your polishing apprenticeship. Consider the following example. It's like if you wanted to build your own house. You wouldn't start building a house without a plan that was drawn up by an architect! It would be a disaster, not precise, and would never be functional. So, it's important to learn the base, and you are doing so. Keep going! The remaining 80% will focus on you doing what you need to do. You can be the smartest book smarts person there is, but until you actually put things into action, by doing it, they will always remain theories to you. Back to building your house. You can have the plans from your architect non-estimated, and never build your house. Guess what. It is not a house then; it's just an idea. You will obtain some of that information here within this book, which will be a great initial start for you. I will also continuously provide additional educational solutions for you as well, on my website at www.LeadershipKing.com, as you continue on your personal journey. You will be able to quickly access the website and start taking advantage of all the bonuses offered to you.

The transformation that you are going through is where you will be creating a vision of change for yourself that connects with you at such a high inspirational level, where you take action with yourself, and with the help of others around you, to make it happen. You are embarking on something that is more than just self-gain. You're creating a movement in which change will occur within you, and because of your willingness to work harder than anyone, you begin to earn the right to influence others around you. You may not think so, but you will see it, feel it, and hear about it.

Think about the following example for a moment. You move away to a country in which you do not speak the language. After immersing yourself in understanding how to read and speak the language, you will be influenced based on the environment you are living in. In other words, if you then go to another area of that country, or a different country where they speak the same language, people will tell you that you have an accent, even if you are speaking the same language! People can sometimes even detect where you are from based on the influence of your accent. Amazing.

Part of your experience in polishing your apprenticeship is understanding some of the different styles of leadership. The big picture concepts are laissez-faire, transactional, and transformational. Laissez-faire usually creates a situation of chaos, lack of structure, and negative outcomes. Most are not satisfied because there is no direction. Think about it. If you were to raise your child in this style, your child would basically learn to fend for him or herself. They would also act out in a way that they self-learned, and most of the time, this is not ideal whatsoever, for many situations. Transactional styles focus on using rewards for good behavior, and punishments for bad behavior. It is definitely more structured than laissez-faire, but this style does not focus on progress. It focuses only on the moment. Transformational leadership focuses on changing the future to inspire followers and accomplish goals. From the beginning of this book, the goal is that you undergo transformational leadership within yourself first. Only then, once you master that concept, and take actions that complement that, transformation will occur in your outside environment as well. We will focus on these characteristics shortly, so that you understand the different components required to make that transformation within your mind, body, and soul. Even though you are graduating from your apprenticeship, you will learn that your coaches and mentors will serve you well, and become your colleagues, as you continue your transformational development.

Polish it....and They Will come

So, now you're ready to make a change?

Before you learn those details, you are going to learn a law from an unchanging science, and how this applies to your life in order to acknowledge how you can change your behaviors to achieve your full potential.

Where to Find a Leadership Polishing Kit

The law I am referring to is known as the law of homeostasis. This means that there is a tendency towards a relatively stable equilibrium between two interdependent elements, especially maintained by physiological processes. A great example of this would be your body temperature. Your body has certain mechanisms that will help control different situations in order to always maintain your temperature to be around 98.6 degrees Fahrenheit. Sweating, shivering, exhaling, and so on are many of the different mechanisms your body will use in order to maintain your body temperature back to this equilibrium (stable state). Take this concept into the world of human behavior, and you will quickly note that human behavior tends to follow the same pattern. When you are in your *comfort zone* or homeostasis, you are in a status quo pattern. In order to achieve your higher level of improvement, you must create a step-by-step approach in order to bring the set homeostasis point to an all-new set level. If you always set the temperature in your home at 68 degrees Fahrenheit, with your proactive decisions and actions, you can set the temperature to a whole new level, and the systems in your house will adjust accordingly to maintain this new set temperature.

Did you ever hear of lottery winners, or nouveau-riche inheritors, that lose all their money, even millions, after only a few years? This is a vivid example where these individuals didn't have a plan, and without a plan, they automatically return back to where their comfort was pre-set in the first place. Poor. Time to change your pre-set, homeostatic level right now.

In this world, what body holds the largest amount of water? If you guessed the OCEAN, you are correct. The OCEAN is huge. Transformational metamorphoses are also huge and, like the OCEAN, they are big and meaningful changes for you and your life. Changes need to occur with you first, and then changes will begin to occur in your outside environment, afterwards, as well. Actually, the word OCEAN is usually used in order to help remember the five personality traits that contribute as characteristics that are necessary in order for you to undergo a transformational change, according to the data findings of Joyce Bono and Timothy Judge, in one of their Meta-Analysis. Simone Phipps later proposed that these 5 traits would be positively related to transformational leadership.

Here they are for you:

Openness to Experience – more accepting of novel ideas, and thereby stimulate your followers intellectually

Conscientious – achievement oriented, so more likely to motivate followers to achieve organizational goals

Extroverted – Outgoing, so good interpersonally and considerate

Agreeable – Pleasant, so good interpersonally and considerate

Neuroticism/emotional stability – Stability makes them better role models to followers and to thoroughly engage them in achieving goals

First things first, though. Polish yourself fully, first. You will learn about the effect on others soon.

Invest to Obtain the Top Leadership Polishing Kit

Who is the first person that comes to your mind when I say the word, *leader*? Perhaps you think of a past or current politician/world leader? Maybe you blurted out the name of a peacemaker or philanthropist?

Where to Find a Leadership Polishing Kit

Throughout all the numerous presentations and workshops that I have done throughout the years, I have never once heard anyone mention themselves as the leader of what they were thinking of.

Why?

Usually, they mention a certain person because this leader is usually representative in emulating the trait characteristics that they *wish* they had. The interesting aspect of the specific exercise, which I have run in my workshops for the past many years, is that all people can become leaders, regardless where you currently are at this moment. Yes, that means you too. Every single person can be a leader. You just have to choose to be a leader, and take the actions necessary in order to make this happen. You may actually think of certain situations where you did so. You are a leader. This involves you mastering actions internally first, and then learning and implementing external leadership behaviors. At this stage, you will learn an overview summary of both, to give you a general idea of the concepts.

Here are a couple of questions for you:

If you had to purchase tires for your child, would you choose a cheap set of tires, or the best quality of tires, knowing that it would save their life?

If you love your child, you would definitely choose the best quality for them, to increase their odds of survival, and to prevent any accident from occurring. Better adhesion = Better odds of braking capability.

If you are facing a life-threatening situation in which you needed a certain medical procedure done, would you pay $50,000, knowing it would save your life, or would you wait 10 years on a waiting list in order to perhaps get the procedure done at no cost?

If you value your life, you would pay for the procedure, hands down. If you do not have the money, you would certainly find ways to creatively fundraise, in order to ensure that you obtain the procedure to save your life.

Obviously, I have used 2 extreme examples here to make a point, yet if these hit and make you hurt right down to your core, then you get it. You have dreams and desires that you want to achieve in this physical life. You can make as many excuses as you want. The reality is, if you are not working on achieving those ultimate dreams right now, and doing whatever it takes to achieve them, you have not fully invested in yourself to obtain the best leadership polishing kit possible. In other words, you need to determine very quickly what you specifically want, and invest in YOURSELF to obtain the book smarts and street-smarts solutions to meet your specific needs and desires. Your life depends on it!!

What are some of the leadership behaviors that you will need to begin mastering once you take action on yourself?

For now, you're going to learn an overview of what I like to refer to as the *Fix 6 Mix*.

These are:

- Shared accountability/transparency
- Cross functional teamwork/collaboration
- Listening/learning
- Benchmarking/continuously improving
- Coaching/developing others
- Business integrity

Where to Find a Leadership Polishing Kit

Shared accountability/transparency means that you act as an owner in everything you do. You take accountability for all actions. If you're working on a project with others, you take joint responsibility (no finger pointing). You have peripheral vision and know everything that's going on around you. You share information freely, in order to make the best decision; therefore, you are highly transparent in your communication, and have a high level of emotional intelligence.

Cross-functional teamwork/collaboration involves delivering a high teamwork performance. No individual alone has all the answers. It involves balancing of the scales, where you accept personal ownership yet work as a team. Everyone in your group must be proactive regardless of position or title.

Listening/learning allows you to encourage and receive constructive feedback, openly share ideas, gain insights, and continuously advance your knowledge and skills. Humility (putting your ego away in your back pocket) ensures the winning idea is expressed, and acted upon. It is not personal. You must learn from each other, as well as your competitors.

Benchmarking/continuously improving drives you to be the best at what you can do. Constantly measure yourself vs. the strongest and highest performing benchmarks, to thereby initially assess yourself candidly. Make positive changes accordingly. Strive for excellence. By you continuously improving, you then create your own benchmark for others to follow. Determine what you and others need, and find solutions to meet those needs.

Coaching/developing others means achieving the highest level of professional excellence. You realize coaching can come from any direction and from anybody, regardless of title. You build the capabilities needed now, energize, and encourage each other, to create a compelling, competitive edge. Everyone

Transform the Coal in your Soul to Diamonds

has coaches, and you should too.

Business integrity simply means you do the right thing. Always follow your moral compass, and you will lead yourself to making the right decision. Always. Be authentic at all times.

WOW! You have just acquired some very important and compelling information that will already change your life. You might now realize it. It's true! You are learning so much already, so imagine what is coming up. I am super excited for you, so keep going! The next chapter will make your head spin with so much excitement that there is no way you will want to stop here. You are a leader. Take the lead, and keep reading.

Chapter 5

Follow the Leader?

"Your time is limited, so don't waste it living someone else's life. Don't be trapped by living with the results of other people's thinking. Don't let the noise of others' opinions drown out your own inner voice. And most important, have the courage to follow your heart and intuition." – Steve Jobs

What is Your Title?

The answer you probably thought of when I asked you what your title is, was most probably what you do for work. Perhaps you have a certain title, such as Administrative Assistant, Vice President of Sales, or Sales Representative. Maybe you responded in such a way as to say it means what you do. Maybe you are a stay-at-home mom/dad, an entrepreneur, or even unemployed.

All those answers are titles or things that describe what you do. The real answer that I'm looking for—and this is very important for you to understand—is what your brand is. You need to be branded, no matter what environment you are currently exposed to, to get into a niche that you are targeting. In simplistic terms, branding makes you unique, and states exactly what your promise is to others. Your brand is derived from who you are as a person, who you want to be, and who

Transform the Coal in your Soul to Diamonds

people perceive you to be. It differentiates you from everyone else.

For example, I will share with you my personal journey so you can get an understanding of what I am referring to. I have been branded as the *Leadership King*. Throughout my lifetime experiences in academics, sports, pharmaceuticals, real estate, and businesses of all kinds, I have been exposed to many different environments. I have been very fortunate to have always polished myself right up to the top, regardless of what situation or environment that I was placed in. For instance, in Academics and Sports, I was captain of my university varsity ice hockey team, received the Most Outstanding Student Award in a university of over 35,000 students, was a 5-time Academic All-Canadian, recipient of the prestigious Guy Lafleur Award of Excellence, as well as many more. In pharmaceuticals, I was awarded the Diamond Award, in which I was the 1st recipient amongst over 20,000 pharmaceutical representatives to do so, as well as a multiple President's Club winner as top representative in Canada in the pharmaceutical industry. I have held positions in sales, marketing, and training, and I have excelled in each position. The reason why I'm sharing this with you is to simply confirm a couple of examples as to why I've been branded as the *Leadership King*.

For you, you will need to brand yourself. There are multiple ways of doing so, of which you and I can further discuss. If you are interested in regards to how to go about doing so, you will have the opportunity to contact me accordingly through my website at www.LeadershipKing.com. In the meantime, you will need to discover some very important things about yourself in order to be defined as a brand. Some of these are:

What do you ultimately stand for? What are your strengths and talents that you are able to offer? How do others perceive

Follow the Leader?

you at this moment? What are some of the qualities that you want others to associate with you?

You really need to stand out, and be unique in multiple ways, in regards to how you're perceived by others. Imagine you are wearing a beautiful pearl necklace. They are all the same in that they are bright and shiny, with a pearly white color. Except one. One of the pearls has an absolutely gorgeous pink hue that is radiant in comparison to all the others. What is the first thing that your eye, or anyone else's, will see when they look at your pearl necklace? Definitely, the gorgeous pink coloured pearl! It's different. It's unique. It's beautiful, and draws attention, versus all the other pearls, which, although beautiful, are exactly the same. It will also be so unique that, most likely, this pink pearl will be centered in the middle of your neck as the show piece for everyone to view. That's powerful! Imagine what will happen when you brand yourself.

At this time, just really understand that titles simply describe what people do. Branding tells everyone who and what you are, what you stand for, and what you're offering. When you brand yourself correctly, you will automatically skyrocket into the top 3% (97% never get there, by the way)! There are other important components to branding, such as a logo, tagline, use of colors, etc. These are all important as a continuation once you are branded.

So, instead of being the same as everyone else in their relentless search for titles (whom I usually refer to as title chasers), you need to define who *you* are. So rather than play follow the leader, start a new line!

Push or Pull?

At first glance, you may think that this is a silly question that has no relevance. Actually, in reality, you will learn very quickly on how this relates to you, and how it makes complete sense. Which one do you think is easier, pushing something or pulling something?

If you ever sat down and watched a strong man competition, you will note that they do some amazing demonstrations of pure strength. Sometimes they do things that simply outright boggle your mind. Maybe you've witnessed someone pulling a truck, a tank, or even an airplane...and doing so with their teeth placed in a mouth guard! On the flip side, you can probably recall these strong competitors pushing certain items too. The only difference is, they are nowhere near pushing the same amount of weight vs. the weight that they can pull. Sometimes, in the workshops that I have done throughout the years, I have the participants do a rope activity, in which they need to push a rope, at the tip, through an obstacle course. Virtually impossible! When I ask them to redo the exercise but have them now pull the rope, by the tip, through the obstacle course, they are able to immediately complete the task. Think about it. Amazing, isn't it?

In marketing, you can have push marketing, or you can have pull marketing. In push marketing, the idea is that you are promoting your products by pushing them onto people. On the other hand, in pull marketing, the goal is to create followers who are loyal, and thereby draw consumers to the products.

Which example would you prefer?

You walk into a department store, and on one side you have a pushy sales representative who is trying to entice you by pushing products in front of you, pushing you to try a sample,

Follow the Leader?

and pushing you to make a quick decision and purchase the product that they are trying to push. Sometimes that sales representative may be bonused on pushing that specific product onto you to thereby increase the visibility of the brand, and hopefully increase their sales. On the other side of the store, you have a similar kind of product (in the same market space), but the major difference is that you've seen information on this brand, you researched the quality of the brand, read amazing testimonials, got positive word-of-mouth referrals, etc. Basically, you are pulled towards the brand because of all of these positive attributes associated with it. On top of that, the sales representative approaches you in a very kind and warm, welcoming way, drawing you in towards the product, and questions your familiarity, usage, and loyalty to that product. Which product would you buy? You probably answered with the second example, where pull marketing was used. So, once again, pull wins over push.

The last example is in terms of you.

What kind of leader do you choose to be? Will you be the kind of person that will push everyone around, like a bully in a playground, forcing your ideas onto others? Or, will you be the kind of person that will be open to listening to others, understanding their points of view, leading as a positive example or model, making decisions on behalf of what is best for the group, etc.?

If you chose the second example of leadership, you are once again choosing the pull method. That is, you are exhibiting such a positive experience, and are such a positive role model, that people are drawn to you. They are being pulled towards you. They gravitate to you. Even the word gravitate has the root word gravity. So, be like the core of the earth, and pull towards you.

Make a conscious effort of pulling the good things towards you and pushing away the negative. As more time passes, people will trust you more, as they are confident in your character as a person.

To Be or Not to Be....Isn't That the Real Question?

You may have noticed that this subtitle slightly resembles what Shakespeare wrote about Hamlet, back in the 1600s, with a little twist. The battle in Hamlet's mind was that he was obsessing about existence, or not, and contemplating the pain of life (which is inevitable), versus the fear of uncertainty of death.

In your case, however, the question is, *to be or not to be*—isn't that the real question?

It's the real question because it's the most important question you can ask yourself. It's basically whether or not you have the courage to be the person you want to be or not. In life, especially in today's ever- connected world, you are constantly being bombarded by thousands and thousands of different messages, beliefs, and influences, from all over and everywhere. The hardest challenge for you, in all of that, is actually knowing what is true and what is not. You have probably seen many examples of fake news being broadcasted, magazines that expose/gossip about people, and so on. The motives of these companies are much more different than what it used to be traditionally. Therefore, you need to be aware of all this, and how, subconsciously and consciously, these influences can affect who you are and how you are.

The best news that I will expose to you at this moment is that you actually get to choose to be or not to be. Every action that you take (or don't take) are decisions that you make. If you are

Follow the Leader?

making those decisions (or not), you are responsible for the outcomes.

For the first time in this book, I am going to ask you to temporarily stop reading. Close your eyes. Take 3 big deep breaths: full inhalation through your nose, full exhalation through your mouth. Now, with your eyes still closed, ask yourself the following 2 questions:

Are you willing to do whatever it takes to be who you want to be? Or, are you going to give up on your true desires, and make excuses to lead a life that is not aligned with what you want to do and who you want to be?

In the end, it's quite fascinating, actually, when I work with people like you in different seminars or workshops. You may think that the answers lie within some sort of a recipe, which is simply applied to your situation. In reality, the answers lie within you. No one else, other than you, is going to decide that for you. Take action. Decide who you want to be. Today. Not tomorrow. Today.

You must be pretty happy to understand what you just read. Perhaps this is the first time that someone is being very authentic with you. Sometimes family, friends, or colleagues from work may tend to water down or sugar-coat any comments or feedback to you in order to protect you from any feelings or emotions. Most people believe that they are helping you by doing so; however, sometimes it can do much more harm. Their intentions are good for you, but the outcomes may be less than desirable.

Think of the following example. You are online, and looking to order a bike. The bike you selected is tailor-made for you, it is the perfect color that you specifically chose, and is a price point that makes sense to you. You enter your credit card information and click the *Buy Now* button. Congratulations, you have just purchased an item that you specifically wanted for yourself. A couple of days go by, and you receive a knock on your front door. Your online package has been delivered! You are super excited, grab a sharp knife, and immediately open up the package. What the...? To your disbelief, an old, used, damaged tricycle with a flat tire was delivered. What would you do? Would you accept it? Of course not! You would do everything in your power to make sure that you received the exact bike that you ordered for yourself since it was specifically tailored to your needs and liking. The same goes for your deepest desires in life. Do not settle for less. Therefore, *to be* is not the real question; it is the real answer. Time to live it out. You earned it!

Earn the Right

For this section, your leadership transformation is going to focus on others for a moment. Earning the right is not something you just do. To earn the right, you must do the right things in a relationship, to earn the privilege to ask or expect something else. It's something you are constantly in the process of doing all the time. Sometimes it won't take much time for you to earn the right, whereas in other situations it can take months, or even decades, in order to gain that privilege. Earning the right is like you obtaining a key that unlocks a special relationship door.

The misconception that is out there is that most people *want* because they want it, and figure they should just get it. It's not that easy. You need to prove yourself in many different ways in order to earn that right with someone. It is only at this stage where you will be able to ask for commitment. It is only here where they will give you permission to enter their circle of influence. I will give you an example of this shortly, but first I want

Follow the Leader?

to share with you certain components that will help you earn the right with people.

You may have learned this one when you were young. Treat people exactly how you want to be treated. Basically, it is all about respect. If you want someone to be prompt, truthful, etc., you need to act in a prompt and honest fashion, at all times, to make that happen. To be the example, you must live and act like the example.

Another component that is important is to make sure that you follow up with all requests, no matter what. For example, anyone who inquires with my real estate business will automatically receive an email response stating that I have received their email. From that point on, I have a 24-hour policy in which my staff provides them with answers and general information to their questions, even if we have *No Vacancy*. The person wants to be acknowledged. You are the same. When you request something of someone, you expect a follow-up response. To earn the right with people, you must consistently do so. You would be surprised how many people say they will follow up, and never do. Do your follow ups, every single time. In today's society, your response to others must be more and more instantaneous since this is where society is currently moving towards, and where this is becoming a minimum expectation to gain entry into the game.

You need to know everything there is to know about other people. Know everything you can, and be proactive in learning about them. Always give as much as you can. Give more than you receive. Be known as a generous giver rather than be known as someone who is a taker.

If you take action and follow some of these concepts, you will build such a solid reputation. You will earn the right to be placed in a more preferable higher level than others. When you have earned the trust from someone, you have earned the right from them.

Here are two different situations that will show the contrast of how the sales cycle has changed and evolved over the years. Imagine you are sales representative. Traditionally, many years ago, a sales person would spend 5% of their time building rapport with someone, 15% of their time qualifying the person, 30% of their time presenting, and 50% closing. Close, close, close. There is an old saying: if you are not selling, you are not closing! With the new current model, you are now spending 50% of your time building trust, 30% of your time on identifying needs, 15% of your time exploring solutions, and the remaining 5% on closing. Big difference! You'll note that the majority of your time needs to be focused on the *building trust* component. Building an authentic relationship is crucial and has to be genuine. You can't fake or pretend at this step. You need to be genuinely interested in the other person.

If you are not trustworthy, not credible, and do not bring added value to someone, you will NOT earn the right to ask for a commitment or be able to move to the next step. This is why, in the new model, it is listed as the most important step to undertake, and where you need to spend most of your time. For example, if you walked into a clothing store and see a clerk on the left of someone you don't know, and then see another clerk on the right of someone you know, trust, and have full confidence in, who are you going to go see? Definitely, the person you know, and the person that has already earned your trust!

You now know that you must do the same thing: earn the right. Create a very strong reputation. Lead by example, and be authentic in learning what is important to other people. If you do this, others will then decide when they will trust and follow you as a result.

Follow the Leader?

Minimum of 2 Choices

Did you ever hear anyone say, "I had no choice?"

If so, from now on, you will now know that this is not true. In every single thing that you do in life, there is always a minimum of 2 choices. For each one of those choices, there is always a corresponding consequence (positive or negative) that goes along with it.

Think about it. For every single decision that you make, you either decide to do so, or you decide not to. Even in the situation where you do absolutely nothing, you still have made the decision to do nothing! As a result of either of the decisions you make, you choose the consequence that goes along with that decision. Therefore, you are always responsible for the decisions you make (or those you don't).

If you understand this concept, you will open up your mind to a whole new level. This is very, very powerful. You now enter into a world where you acknowledge that there are no excuses. If you take this concept and act upon it, you have now proactively escaped the world of being a victim and entered into a world of productive mastery.

Here's an analogy that will make sense to you. Imagine you are on a movie set and the film that is being created is on *Your Life.* If you choose to be an actor in that movie, you will listen to the director and act in consequence to what you're being told to do. If you choose to be the director, you choose to direct how you want your life movie to be directed, and the vision on how it would be produced. If this movie is about your life, you will definitely want to be sitting in the director's chair! You know exactly what you want and need in life, to make a proactive decision to direct the steps needed to obtain the highest quality movie about your life ever created. Create your own autobiography. Every day.

Not only do you have a minimum of two choices, you also have a minimum of two kinds of decisions. On one side, you have decisions that are not easily reversible. Those decisions, when taken, need to be well thought-out in regards to what kinds of consequences occur as a result of making those important decisions. On the other side, you have decisions that you can make and easily reverse quite quickly. In essence, it is almost like you are testing the market, or your theory, to see what kind of response (consequence) you get as a result of that decision. Once you have gathered enough information, you can quickly alter your decision accordingly and continue to test the response, and adjust along the way.

So, if you think back to the title of this chapter, *Follow the Leader?*, it should now be much clearer for you. Most people will choose or follow someone blindly, or be influenced by others. That is not a bad thing if the intentions are good, and if this aligns with your core beliefs. You have learned, as the leader you now are, that you have the right to decide what is best for you. You have the right to take your *soul diamonds* and make sure that they shine as bright as can be!

Inside Out

There are different models that you can utilize in order to become a leadership king in your ultimate goal, or in whatever area you want to become, in order to take you right to the top. The fastest way for you to get there is going to be by using this *Inside-Out* approach. This means that in order to make changes to bring you where you want to be, it all starts within yourself first: your inner thoughts, your inner feelings, and actions that

Follow the Leader?

will have a direct influence in regards to these items. These are all within your control and decision-making capabilities.

Upon mastering your inside world, you will begin to influence and have a spillover effect into your *Outside* environment. As your outside world continues to grow and expand, and you continue to optimize your inside world, you will begin to see a far-reaching exponential growth everywhere.

You are going to need to understand the differences in perceptions that each brings out. In regards to your inner world, it is only you that is able to perceive and judge yourself. All the perceptions you create on how you *see* or *feel* about yourself are judged solely by you. No one will be able to judge you in regards to these aspects because there is no way for them to understand exactly how you feel, or see yourself internally. On the flip side, everyone in your outside world will make judgements about you based on what they see you exhibiting from your outside actions. For example, you may have a frown on your face. One person from the outside may perceive that you are not pleased. Another person may perceive you as being sad. They are making these perceptions based on what you are displaying from the outside. Internally, you may be feeling full of gratitude, and frowning based on how appreciative you are for everything around you. Completely different! You see, there are major differences in regards to the perceptions internally versus the perceptions others have of your *outside*. It's very important you continue to grow from inside out. The reason is that your actions will all be based on what you are really trying to attain, versus trying to simply *act* in order to please other people's perceptions of you.

There are different forms of how you communicate with others. There is verbal, written/visual, and non-verbal. Verbal

Transform the Coal in your Soul to Diamonds

communication is where you listen to a person to understand their meaning. Written communication is where you read or view to understand the meaning. Lastly, non-verbal is where you observe a person and infer meaning. Guess which form of communication you utilize, and which says the most to someone? Believe it or not, it's non-verbal communication!

Actually, this has been studied extensively. If all types of communication equals 100%, what do you think is the breakdown between the three types of communication?

As surprising as it may seem, only 7% of someone's understanding of your message is based on your actual words; 38% is based on your visual delivery (tone, pace, volume of speech, etc.), and the remaining 55% is based on your non-verbal body language. What you don't say, is actually the most important. Think of how important this is in a job interview, or when you are being questioned at any border crossing, or how you act when you're performing your day-to-day job. Therefore, be aware of how you appear since your outside world is constantly making judgments of you, based on that. When you first walk into a room for an interview, it can usually take 2–4 seconds for someone to make their initial judgment of you, and you haven't even spoken a word yet!

You are moving at an incredible pace, and your transformational mindset is continuing to progress. Keep your learnings going, and move on to the next chapter right away to learn more about mastering becoming a proactive/active pro master—incredible learnings that are life changing. Go, go, go!

Chapter 6

ProActive = ActivePro

"A man who views the world the same at fifty as he did at twenty, has wasted thirty years of his life." – Muhammad Ali

Become a Solution Specialist

There was a theory in the 1300s that was described by William of Occam. It was termed Occam's razor. Basically, the suggestion is, the simpler a theory is, the better. If two theories predict phenomena to the same accuracy, then the one which is simpler is the better one. In other words, if there are additional aspects of a theory, which doesn't in any way, shape, or form increases its predicting ability, they are therefore unnecessary, and should be stripped away. Your life is to determine the most efficient path in achieving your goals or specific needs. There may be many alternative paths, or more complex paths, in order to achieve your result. You need to analyze, plan, and work towards choosing the most time efficient and simpler version. Any distractions or complexities that alter you from achieving your results in the most optimized fashion need to be stripped away. You need to use *Occam's razor* and shave away what is not needed.

Let's take a look at an example. Look at Google's homepage. What do you see? You see Google's name at the top and underneath the name is a search box. That's it. Nothing

Transform the Coal in your Soul to Diamonds

more than that really. There is no advertising or links anywhere near the Google name and the search box. The screen is pretty well white, bright, and clean shaven from any other distractions, other than the Google name and search box. There is no clutter whatsoever around the name and search box. Google's homepage and intention is that they are a search engine to help you find exactly what you want. There is no other distractions or advertising to draw you away from their specific solution for you. It is with a razor's edge precision that they offer this specific solution to your needs. If you need to search something, Google is the search engine specialist that will find a solution to your needs!

I'm going to share another personal story with you. When I was working in the pharmaceutical industry for many years, people would ask me what I did for a living. My response was very consistent and precise. I would answer that I was a solution specialist for patients and doctors. In other words, I didn't say that I was a sales representative, product specialist, or business account manager, etc. I was a solution specialist. This answer actually did not change when I held the role in marketing, or when I was in a training role. I was always working at becoming the top specialist and finding solutions that matched the function of my different roles.

Take a moment and think about your current situation. What are you doing right now from a work perspective? Personal? Social?

You see, you need to be reflective and understand what you do in these different settings, and what your goal or purpose is in regards to them. You don't want to be among the average and simply go through the motions without thinking what you really want. Others do that all the time. Decide to be different, right

ProActive = ActivePro

now. Actually, you are! You know that because you're reading this book, and you are looking to polish yourself right up to the top. You learned to prioritize and work on your ultimate life goal as being the most important priority. Become a solution specialist on all the steps required in order for you to achieve that. You have just read that you can be a solutions specialist for your other interests as well. Become a solution specialist in those different areas. You should start to begin to notice a common theme. Become a solution specialist in everything you do!

You will notice that even a marginal increase in your actions will have a tremendous amplification of your results. You see this all the time in different sporting settings. For example, a professional golfer can change his coach, tweak their golf swing in a certain way, work their psychological game, etc., and all of these actions propel the golfer to the top. At the top, the difference in the results of the prize money is not marginal, however; it is a huge difference, based on those marginal improvements.

Become a solution specialist in your thoughts, feelings, actions, and decisions. Even if you make marginal changes, the results will be astounding. Any solution you provide will progress you closer and closer to the top!

Practice Practicing and become a Pro

It's quite amazing when you think about what the definition of a professional really is. The word, *professional,* has so many different meanings. You may think that a professional is someone who holds a profession in what traditionalists call *white-collar* professions, like a doctor or a lawyer. Or, perhaps you think a professional is someone who is being paid to play a sport of the highest ranks possible. For example, a baseball pro, football pro, ice hockey pro, or professional race car driver, etc. You could probably provide hundreds of different examples in different sports or white-collar professions.

But, wait.

Is being a pro only applicable to those *traditional* perceptions of what the definition of a pro is?

The answer is a definite NO. You can become a pro in anything you embark in. You may be thinking that there is no way you can become a pro in such and such. The answer is, yes you can. Let me share with you what I mean.

There's a quote I came up with, which I always say. *Habit is the practice of practicing.* In other words, practice practicing, and become a pro at what you do. The barriers you may create in your mind are that you perhaps think that you do not have the talent in order to achieve a pro status. If you think that, you are further from the truth. Your evaluation needs to come from within you. The issue is that most people will compare themselves to others in regards to how they perceive themselves, or whether they are a pro in what they do, versus others.

Why?

You live in a competitive world where society has created what society believes is the norm. If you think about it, everything that is considered *normal* in society is based on what society has determined that *normal* to be! You are thereby always being compared to what society believes is poor, average, and superior. That will never change in the physical world. People are always comparing and creating competitions to show who the best is, etc. This is WAY different on how you should be with yourself. What you can control, is how you think, feel, and act,

ProActive = ActivePro

and in regards to what you want to achieve in your inner world. Practice practicing in becoming a pro, to the level and standard that you determine for yourself! Nobody knows that standard except you. Become the best pro at being a parent, friend, sibling, colleague, citizen, and so on. You set your own standards, and you practice practicing the necessary solutions that you require in order to become the pro you deserve to be, in what you are wanting to achieve. You could be a pro concierge, a pro administrative assistant, etc. Just like you can be a professional stay-at-home parent, or professional doctor. You set your own standards as to what being a pro is. Practice practicing, and create the habit of professionalism in everything you do.

Having said all of this, you should now feel very motivated to act upon your dreams and desires. You have certain strengths and qualities within you that are absolute treasures. Extract your soul diamonds and polish them to their shiniest, most blinding state possible. Be proactive in becoming your own active pro. Exploit your strengths to their maximum.

In the physical world, society will, most of the time, remunerate the best or highest producing professionals. Indeed, some are born with a certain natural talent. You may have also seen certain individuals who had natural talents, but they made some bad decisions, or allowed their talent to wither away because they didn't practice practicing good habits. On the other hand, there are others who have had to practice practicing their art in order to achieve the highest levels that they could achieve. Certain professional athletes play a full career in the highest professional leagues, in which they were never drafted (an organized process that allows teams to obtain the rights of a player). They basically earned their spot as an unrestricted free agent, or in some other way. A surprising fact on someone who was never drafted....Wayne Gretzky! He is someone whom most will undoubtedly consider the best and most productive ice hockey player to play in the NHL. Yet he was never drafted!

You could read numerous stories on how some professional athletes have dedicated so much of their time to practicing their skills, that they become an automatic habit. For example, Odell Beckam Jr. is a professional football player for the New York Giants in the National Football League. He practices catching the football with one hand so many times, in so many different awkward positions, that when it comes time to execute that habit, he catches the ball with one hand. He's on highlight reels almost weekly, making amazing one handed catches. He has done this so many times that when others do it, they are referred to Odell Beckam Jr., almost all the time. Habit is the practice of practicing. Set your own standards.

Aerodynamic Theory

If you want to get to where you want to go, put your sails directly into the winds of time, and you will notice your boat will move that much faster.

Streamline everything that you do in life, and be as efficient as you can be. You do this, and you will be well on your way to success. I like to refer to this as your *aerodynamic theory*.

What do I mean by this?

Next time you're driving in your car, and you are going at a certain speed (make sure that there is no traffic of course!), stick your arm out into the wind. Place your arm in a horizontal position, with your palm facing down, and your fingertips pointing towards the front. Feel how easy your arm and hand cuts through the resistance of the wind. Now, quickly place your hand and arm in the vertical position so that your palm is facing forward, and your fingertips are facing the sky. Immediately, your arm will fly backward, and you will have to work extra hard just to fight against the resistance.

Let's take this example and relate it to your life.

You will need to streamline your efficiency and target your goals. Cut through any kind of resistance that is holding you back. In contrast, if you decide not to work on yourself, or have no goals, or choose to constantly focus on the negative aspects of life (being a victim), you will evidently never get to where you want to go, or if you do, you will be far behind the rest of the crowd. This is a law of life.

There are infinite examples in regards to the aerodynamic theory. Race cars undergo extensive testing within wind tunnels in order to optimize and streamline the resistance from the wind. If you are older, you will recall that internet once ran through a *dial-up* fashion, versus today's highly efficient, ultra-high-speed internet that is able to download tremendous amounts of data so quickly. The term is even called *streaming.* Swim with the current if you want to swim faster! If you worked in calculating certain formulas many years ago, you would have needed to input the data and push the enter button, and allow the computer processor the full weekend in order to calculate the answer! Now, the calculation takes milliseconds.

You see, all processes and applications in life are trending towards being the most efficient and aerodynamic as possible, in order to bring you from A to B in the most efficient fashion. The area that you can control for yourself is that which happens within your own mind. So many barriers are placed onto you from others, as well as those you impose upon yourself, that all of those things can hinder your aerodynamic capabilities. You are reading this book in hopes to find your way in becoming a leadership king at what you want to do, so that you can polish yourself right to the top. Keep reading, learning, and applying your knowledge to continuously streamline your thoughts, feelings, and actions. You will thereby create the most aerodynamic results. Keep doing so. Act today. There is no need for you to wait until everything is perfect in order to achieve what you want to achieve. If you think that, you are using it as an excuse to lie to yourself. Start streamlining yourself today. Allow yourself to apply this theory to achieve your goals.

The aerodynamic theory is having its effect in your outside world, whether you like it or not. The world wants everything, yesterday. The millennials search for instant gratification and are known to change jobs if they don't get what they want immediately. Waiting at a crosswalk, seeing the countdown of seconds going down, feels like an eternity. Life is moving at lightning speeds. You are in the transformational era. You also have the right to achieve what you deeply desire in this physical life. You are in the best era, with the most tools available at your fingertips to find solutions to your needs. You just need to take the leap of faith to proactively go for your dreams, and know that the decision is ultimately yours to make.

When I'm speaking to a room or a convention full of people, I am very fortunate in that I know those in attendance (like those such as yourself reading this book) are taking the initial step in working towards aerodynamically streamlining their lives. Congratulate yourself, as you are conscious of your desires and are doing something about it. You are also responsible for what you do with that information. You know you can count on me for continuing to provide as much education, and as many solutions to everyone, to meet their own needs as much as possible. You need to count on yourself in order to take proper action.

ProActive = ActivePro

Inertia Overhaul

You are going to overhaul inertia. You're going to take whatever energy you are required to drum up and overcome inertia to make things happen.

I learned a very interesting formula, at a recent parent's meeting, from the professor of my daughter's 6th grade class. She was talking to us about the concept of $R = E * S$, which they learned, and they were going to apply throughout the year with the students. Basically, Results = Effort * Strategies. So, to get the results you are looking for, it is going to require your effort, as well as all the different strategies you apply, in order to achieve the results you are looking to achieve.

One of the strategies you are going to need to understand is in regards to the equation of continuity. In science terms, this is an equation that states that a fluid flowing through a pipe flows at a rate which is inversely proportional to the cross-section area of the pipe. In simpler terms, if we constrict the pipe, the fluid will flow faster. In contrast, if we open up the pipe to be much larger, the fluid flows at a slower rate. Think of this in terms of a beer keg. You open the spout (the small tube), and beer comes rushing out at a certain speed. If you were to look inside the barrel, however (the big tube), where the size is much wider than the width of the spout, you would notice that the speed of the beer barely moved in comparison to that of the spout. Actually, you probably wouldn't even see the speed or level of beer change too much. How this relates to you and the real world is that it is very important for you to streamline your goals, and focus on the most important tasks at all times. Having you focus specifically on your most important goal, you will *constrict the tube*. This, in turn, will accelerate all your energy, and provide you with a specific targeted strategy that is important to you, and thereby provide you maximum results. Obviously, by implementing this kind of thinking, you will move towards attaining your goals much faster. You will be taking steps right to the top.

Another concept you are to be aware of is the superposition principle. This is, in general, when a number of influences are acting on a system, the total influence on that system is merely a sum of the individual influences. When you think of this principle, break down the word superposition into two words: *super* and *position*. Basically, after taking into consideration all the positive and negative aspects that occur throughout your journey, when added together, what is your super position? In mathematical terms, the influences of the principles would be added linearly. For example, 4 - 1 = 3, or 1 + 1 = 2. However, in the real world, we know that this concept exists; however, some influences are more *heavily weighted* then other influences.

Think of the following situation. Imagine you are 13 years old. You are on a playground, and you notice that there are 5 teens and 1 bully. The 5 teens each tell you to do the same one positive thing, yet the bully forces you to do another. In this situation, the bully (n=1) might unfortunately force an outcome much different than the greater number of positive influences (n=5). Then again, maybe not. It depends on your decision as to what to do in that situation. Regardless, a number of influences will exist in your life, and once again, you decide which influences you will choose to add together.

So, now, what is 1 + 1?

You should be able to confidently attribute any number here, and your answer will be correct. In simplest terms, by focusing on your specific life plan, you decide your own ultimate results. To go even a step further, by surrounding yourself with talented, positive people (after you work on your own self), this will help

ProActive = ActivePro

you exponentiate any results deemed possible in your mind. By doing so, you are overhauling inertia to infinite levels.

Present Yourself with a....Present!

Have you ever given yourself a present?

You will do so today. The present you will give yourself, is yourself. You are who you are. You are at where you are at. This cannot be changed, as it has already happened. Giving yourself, to yourself, is the best present that you can give. And the present you are giving is *in the present*. Meaning, today. At the present time.

The incredible aspect in all this is that if you look at the word *present*, it is made up of two words: *pre* and *sent*. The gift you're giving yourself is something that you are *pre-sent*-ing to yourself. In other words, the results you will achieve at the end of the time line, which you have set for yourself to achieve your goals, will all be a result of the actions and the decisions you are making at this specific time. The past cannot be changed, but actions you take at the present time will shape the outcome of your future—*pre sent* all to yourself. Be the hero in your own movie.

Do you know how much it costs per year to attend Harvard?

Without financial aid, the tuition for the 2016–2017 year was $43,280 USD. A four-year program would cost you $173,120 USD.

Do you find this to be worth it?

In reality, there is no answer to that. You may have a point of view in which the value you receive in exchange is worth way more than that amount. On the other end of the spectrum, you might think that paying that amount is absolutely outrageous. In the end, the wonderful aspect is that you have the freedom of making decisions.

The present you are to give to yourself today is actually that of life. Your life. The gift you are unwrapping today is your most inner desires. Accept it. Cherish it. Take care of it, as it is your most valuable possession. Feel it to the fullest possible emotion you have ever felt. You deserve it and are born into this physical life to use it to your maximum potential. Without it, you cannot provide to others.

You will undergo life-changing experiences as you continue to read this book. You will take action towards attaining what you want for you and your loved ones. You will give yourself the gift of life by consciously choosing to do whatever you need to do to obtain it.

If you need to invest in yourself, ensure you are doing so with a clear goal in mind, to obtain the maximum value in regards to both your street smarts and book smarts. The highest performing individuals at the top all have coaches, and this relates to any discipline or industry. If you have a boss who is not providing you an environment to grow towards where you want to grow, listen to your *inside boss* (your mind and soul), and find a coach that will help guide you on your journey.

You can visit as many stores as possible to try to find the perfect gift for yourself. You will note very quickly that your ultimate gift cannot be found in a store. The perfect gift is the life you create for yourself.

ProActive = ActivePro

Which League are You Playing In?

In every league, whether it's little league or the big league, there are always a set of rules that govern them. These rules are there to create a standard for which everyone looking to participate has to abide by. These leagues, and those who participate, are aware of the criteria required in order to play.

You need to determine which league you are willing to play in. Since you have the choice to decide, you will need to understand the rules of engagement in that league. This means, in order to reach the top, you need to understand the playing field that you are wanting to play in. You can change leagues at any time you want, or change what kind of league you're playing in. If you really want, you can even create your own league!

Basically, if you really think about it, you can decide what you want to do in life, and if it doesn't exist, you can create it. You can decide to be an employee, a business person, an investor, or even an entrepreneur. You decide what league you want to play in. As the title of this chapter indicates, you must be *proactive* in what you do, in order to be an *active pro,* in whatever league you are signing up to play in. If you want to create your own league, do so. Remember, like some of these participants, you can sign a contract for however long you want. You can ask for a trade. Maybe you will retire and move into a whole new role within the organization. Maybe you will start your own league!

Here's an example of creating your own league.

Who is credited for creating the World Wide Web?

Tim Berners-Lee is credited as the individual who invented the World Wide Web. The web is actually a way of accessing

Transform the Coal in your Soul to Diamonds

data online in the form of web sites and hyperlinks. The www was created in 1989, and helped launch the internet, which almost everyone uses on a daily basis, in order to access all kinds of information! Could you function without internet in today's world? Probably not! It's incredible to think that it was also created less than 30 years ago.

Use all of this information and integrate it within yourself. If it is your goal to do nothing, do little, or fear to go after your most ambitious goals, then you are deciding to play in a little league. That's okay, if that's what you want. You assume the consequences of your decision.

Since you're reading this book, however, you know that you are not looking to play in the little leagues. They already have enough players. Too many players! Aim for the big leagues, and become the *proactive active pro* that you are.

If you still don't think you are a leader at this stage, then look out for the next chapter! You will learn to soar to a whole new level, and even do so without realizing it. Now, that's exciting! Keep reading, and fly onto the next chapter.

Chapter 7

Leadership is for the Birds

"Leadership is a choice, not a position." – Stephen Covey

Who's Leading?

Did you ever read about a stock report, or something within the newspaper, only to realize that at that point, it's already too late? This is why it's called the *news,* because it already happened, and if you didn't create it, you probably won't benefit from it. You should be asking yourself: "Where are all the leaders? Who's leading?" This is where you see a difference between taking the initiative to accomplishing tasks early on, versus allowing yourself to be caught amongst the masses. A good friend of mine always told me that you're always in second place if you're chasing! Step out, and be a leader. Don't wait for someone to give you a title. Be a leader today. That starts by you taking action, earlier than later. You know what your ultimate dreams and goals are; so, at this moment, right now, act and optimize your beliefs.

Let's talk about an example that I use quite often within my presentations and coaching sessions. The title of this chapter says that leadership is for the birds. You may look at this title and view it in a negative way, where you imagine that leadership is not worth it.....that it's for the birds. You may also, on the other hand, by simply reading this book and being so far along already in your journey, view this statement as saying that leadership can be learned from the actions of what birds do.

Birds are incredible creatures. The example I'm going to refer to here is a kind of bird called the Canada goose. If you have the opportunity to view them live, you will note that they fly as a flock but do so in a V formation. This is not by accident. In order to save their energy, they fly in this formation. They can actually fly 70% further than if they were to fly alone, since they take advantage of the drafting that takes place in relation to the air resistance that they face.

Did you also know that they take turns leading at the head of the V?

Each goose takes their turn to become the *leader,* as they all understand that each and every one of them is a leader. The fact is, these Canadian geese rotate in a fashion where the goose that is leading the V is the one that is taking all the initial air resistance, and has to work harder than the rest of his colleagues within that V formation. When the head goose, who has stepped up and taken the lead, begins to fatigue, another goose will step up and take the lead, in order for his colleague to file back into the formation and take advantage of the drafting that occurs due to this V formation. You see the same strategy applied if you ever watch certain sporting events, such as cycling, race car driving, marathon running, etc. The other interesting point in all of this is that these Canadian geese even honk numerous times in order to cheer each other on, as well as fly in such a way to maintain their strategic vision, in order to fully communicate with each other.

So how does this apply to you?

You have to consciously realize that you have leadership abilities that are within you. Leadership is not attributed to a title. There are examples around you such as Gandhi, Mother Teresa, and so on. You have the same opportunities to step out and proactively make the decision to do whatever you need to do to attain your deepest desires. Birds fly in a V formation to maximize their individual efforts, and to utilize a strategy collectively as a group, to achieve a common goal. You could try to fly alone if you so choose to; however, you will fatigue quite quickly, as you will have to take all the resistance on yourself at all times.

Think about it. All the items that you utilize in your everyday life were created by someone who took the initiative to follow their dream and create accordingly. You are a leader. You decide when you want to step up and take action. That's the first step. If you omit this step, you are most probably never going to achieve what you truly want. Once you decide to take action for yourself, the next step lies within harmonizing this within a system, and leveraging that system to its maximum efficiency.

It's Not Only About the "I", It's About the "V"!

You may have heard of the saying, "There is no 'I' in TEAM." You would be correct to assume that this usually holds true. When you first look at the statement, you will notice that the letter 'I' is indeed not part of the word, *TEAM*. On the other hand, all teams are made of individuals. It is the contribution of each individual within that team setting that will make the collective difference.

Hence, I like to share the concept more in regards to, *it's not only about the "I," it's about the "V!"*

Transform the Coal in your Soul to Diamonds

From the moment you wake up in the morning, you are taking action on numerous decisions, which are usually automatic. For instance, you wake up, take a shower, get dressed, have breakfast, brush your teeth, etc., and the list goes on. You may think that you are doing all these actions for yourself. However, when you really think about it, you are probably taking actions that are more aligned to the "V". When you are conscious of this, you will notice that so many more things happen harmoniously, as well as see that other things are also getting done.

Imagine you are 13 years old. You wake up from your bed, take a shower, and get dressed. The clothes you are putting on are clean, as a result of your parents taking action to ensure you have clean clothes to wear on your way to school. You go downstairs to have breakfast, and notice that your older sister has taken the initiative to cook the whole family a wholesome, healthy breakfast. In return, you say to your parents that you will make your own lunch, so that they can have the time to prepare themselves for work and, at the same time, you will make your older sister's lunch as well, since you are already doing this for yourself. This is an example of not only being about the "I" but more about the "V." You are directly acting as an individual; however, you are contributing to the collective goals. Everyone is working to help each other out, versus each person trying to do all things on their own.

This concept can be applied to many different situations. At work, more than likely, you have a certain *title* that depicts your responsibilities and what you are confined to do. You should realize, now that you are a proactive leader, titles do not define who you are. Yes, you have responsibilities in delivering on the role you have been hired for, yet you do not have to restrict yourself only to that. You have the choice. You can decide to stay average and simply go through the motions for the role you play.

That's okay, if you want to be average. This is a choice that only you can make. If you are looking to progress and become a leadership king by polishing yourself right up to the top, you will look for ways to optimize and contribute, above and beyond your current role, and find ways to optimize your individual efforts to the collective group. Your actions will get noticed. There are also times where, although you may want to act, you will need to trust your team to fulfill their actions and step up in helping you.

Let's look at a sporting example for that situation. Imagine you are playing the game of ice hockey. You are on the ice and, unfortunately, the referee calls a penalty on you. You now have to go sit in the penalty box for a minimum of two minutes, and watch your team continue to play, with one person down. In other words, the other team has a one person advantage (Power Play), while your team is down a player (Penalty Kill) for those 2 minutes. During that time frame, you do not want the other team to score, and encourage your teammates to kill off the penalty. Your coach takes the decisions required to put the best individuals in their respective roles, to obtain the best results. At times, you will be penalty killing, while at other times you will be on the power play, and sometimes in the penalty box or on the bench, trusting your team to work to collectively reach your common goals. If you think about it, when it comes to statistics in ice hockey, someone who scores a goal is worth the same as an assist from the 1 or 2 people who passed them the puck. Both contributions are individually different but collectively reach the "V" objective. You can decide which role to play, and hone your skills accordingly. By reading this book, you now fully know that your proactive leadership will contribute to your "I," as well as look to have it also contribute to your "V," if you want maximum results.

Transform the Coal in your Soul to Diamonds

Birds of a Feather DO Flock Together

You have just been exposed to understanding the concept of the flying V formation that Canadian geese choose to do in order to maximize their energy, their strategy in terms of the rotational leadership, and their encouragement in communication by their honking to one another. So, you can now add the next concept: birds of a feather DO flock together.

You will see ample examples of this across all different situations, industries, and what I like to call *actual human living experiments* (a.k.a., reality TV). It is amazing to note that in most reality TV shows, where there is a competitive aspect, people will automatically create certain groups, tribes, teams, or partners, in order to create a commonality based on their similarities. The beliefs and attitudes of these groups that are formed, are based on something familiar to that group, which unites them in such a way that they will bond with each other rather quickly. You need to be aware that this behaviour occurs all the time in your current surroundings. Let's look at a couple of other examples together.

Imagine you are back in high school. What group did you associate yourself with? Were you part of the jocks? The nerds? The weirdos?

You could probably answer that question in a matter of seconds! It is normal that you would associate yourself amongst a group where all of you shared similar values and outlooks of life. This is what you find interesting, and as a result, you like this group. You want to be part of this group. It's not like you dislike the other groups. It's simply that you prefer to spend time with people who are interesting to you. You do the same thing at work, and with your close group of friends you make, as well as in your love life. In choosing your lifelong soulmate, you attempt to align with someone who is very similar to yourself. Birds of a feather DO flock together.

Now that you understand this, in order to reach the top, you need to understand who your audience is. If you are looking into tapping into a new market, building a relationship with an important client, or perhaps simply trying to expand your knowledge regarding other points of view, so that you can understand why others choose and make decisions based on their common values—whatever your reasons may be—you need to think, feel, and understand the reasons that make others choose the decisions they make.

There is a word of caution you will need to be aware of. You are not out there to manipulate anyone or take advantage of a situation, because you are now conscious of the other people's beliefs and attitudes. You do this so that when it comes time to meeting the needs of that other person, group, team, or company; you know exactly what they are wanting and, thereby, find a solution that is specific to their needs. You must be *fully* genuine, authentic, and compassionate about helping that other group further progress. This is not a selfish game. You are taking these actions for the greater purpose of all parties.

You should be absolutely amazed now that, even just after reading the past couple of paragraphs, you will start to see the disassociation regarding certain situations. Think of a relationship that is not going well, and you will note that their individual interests or values are most of the time not aligned, or have changed over time. Remember, your interactions and relationships are dynamic in nature. They are not static. They change and evolve continuously. You may have been part of the gothic group in high school, whereas now you are fully immersed in being with individuals who have a similar business-like mindset. You are always evolving, and will continue to be a part of different groups, with similar interests to yourself, throughout different eras of your lifetime. You are now conscious of this. Moving forward, you are to choose what *feathers* you wish to wear.

The media, marketing, and advertisements will attempt to shape you and influence you all the time. That is their role. The government, your company, and your boss will want to shape you into their culture. If your company has values, or takes actions that are not aligned with your beliefs, you have the option to either stay or leave. Either you choose to stay and work on influencing the current environment, or you leave to find another company that meets your internal values.

Do the following exercise: find someone who is absolutely passionate about their job. Ask them questions as to why they are so passionate in what they do. You will uncover some amazing information regarding their alignment, as well as their desire in being part of that group. Next, find someone who absolutely hates what they do. Notice the differences in their demeanour, the language they use, their non-verbal, the words they say, etc. Those people are living of a *different feather* than their deepest desires.

Your transformation begins now. You are now conscious of these aspects and, moving forward, will make decisions to find your feathers, so that you can flock together with others of the same interests.

Communication Stimulation

You learned in a previous chapter that the breakdown of the different types of communication splits into verbal (7%), visual delivery such as tone of voice, etc. (38%), and non-verbal (55%). Hence, you communicate in these fashions all the time. This will help you understand how you communicate with others, and vice versa. You are now going to learn other aspects in regards to the stimulation of communication.

Did you know that you can speak anywhere between approximately 125–200 words per minute? Yet you can listen to approximately 500 words per minute. Are you surprised by this? The easiest way you can remember this is that you have one mouth but two ears. Listening is a skill that you will need to master, in order to become a leadership king in whatever you wish to achieve. To go one step even further, empathetic listening is the ultimate pinnacle skill required.

How does this apply to you?

The fact that your brain can listen to more words per minute, versus speaking more words per minute, creates a situation where, if you are not fully engaged and concentrating on really listening to the person or people in front of you, you may find yourself being distracted, and wander off in your mind. If that's the case, you will miss certain pertinent information that the other person is communicating with you— you know, that feeling where you're listening to someone, and then, all of a sudden, your mind wanders, and you have no idea what they have said in the last 30 seconds. That's exactly the case! Your brain can get bored and start thinking of other things. That's why empathetic listening is so important to help you get right to the top. It takes work, concentration, and the ability that you really focus all your energy on the interaction that you are having at that present time. Always be present to them, and listen intently. The skill is so important because it allows you to fully understand the meaning of the other person.

Let's take it even another step further. You learned the different forms of communication, and how important empathetic

Transform the Coal in your Soul to Diamonds

listening is to you, so that you can really understand the needs of the person in front of you. Now you are going to learn how to adjust your approach to the personality style of the individual in front of you.

To make this very simple and applicable to you, most people display characteristics within a personality style that can be described using 4 different colours. Most of the time, people exhibit a mix of these different personality traits. However, you will notice that most will have a primary colour trait.

The four colours are red, blue, green, and yellow. Below, you will learn a summary breakdown of what characterizes each of these colours.

On a bad day, someone who is *red* is associated with behavioural traits of someone who is aggressive, controlling, and intolerant. On a good day, red is somebody who is competitive, demanding, and determined. Therefore, when you are communicating with someone who is more of a primary red, you must get to the point. Short, concise answers are usually what most red individuals are searching for. If you give them a 2-page response, you will immediately lose them. You will also notice, in other ways, who is a typical red. For instance, someone who is red usually always emails you in very short, 1 or 2 sentences. Now, knowing what you know, adjust your communication style, and respond to them in very short, 1 or 2 sentences. Adjust yourself to their preferred style!

On a bad day, someone who is *blue* is indecisive, suspicious, and reserved. On a good day, a blue is cautious, precise, and questioning. Basically, someone who is blue usually wants to find out all the specific, minute details about something, and is rather quite analytical. Your response to a blue? You need to usually provide lots of facts, and be exact in your responses....to the decimal point! You know the term, *analysis by paralysis*? Most of the time, these are individuals who are *blue*.

As for green, on a bad day, a *green* usually displays characteristics where they are docile, bland, and reliant, whereas on a good day, they are very caring, encouraging, relaxed, and patient. Most of the time, you will notice that a green doesn't really open or express their emotions. Therefore, you should never put them on the spot, as they like to prepare in advance. Someone who is more predominantly green definitely appreciates being recognized for their competence and ideas. You will have to realize that they won't come shouting this out to you. They are calm and very insightful, and you will notice that they have great ideas. You will just need to recognize that, so you will have to nurture them a bit, in order to help them take action.

Last, but not least, someone who is *yellow* will display excitable, frantic, indiscreet behaviour on a bad day, whereas on a good day, someone who is yellow is sociable, dynamic, and enthusiastic. If you are dealing with someone who is yellow, you need to be happy and passionate, and communicate and positively assure them all the time. You will want to avoid bogging these people down with all the details or being pessimistic. A yellow is excited about their dreams, and likes to be involved, so be that way when you are dealing with someone who displays yellow characteristics.

You will obviously not be able to acquire all these different skills immediately, in terms of adjusting to your audience in front of you. At this stage, you are simply learning to be aware that most people fit within a mix of these characteristics, and usually have a primary colour. You are gaining your knowledge foundation by reading this book. For future and more advanced learning, you will be able to continue your journey by going to my website at www.LeadershipKing.com.

Does the Early Bird *Really* Get the Worm?

The answer to this question is an absolute *yes*. The early bird, really getting the worm, doesn't just refer to the fact that if you wake up early in your day, you will be able to get so much more done in comparison to someone who wakes up 2 hours later than you. It refers to other meanings as well. Even further to that, it is not to compare versus someone else. If you decide to take action and wake up 1 hour earlier in your day, you will be able to tackle *performing actions* that will be life-changing. For example, if you decided to wake up 1 hour earlier, every day, and applied cardiovascular and strengthening exercises into this time slot, you would have increased energy, changes to your physical body, and improvement in your psychological mindset through the release of natural chemicals (i.e., endorphins) in your body. An extra hour a day to do something for yourself equates to over 15 days that you have given yourself for that! This is just an example. You can decide what you dedicate to this 1 hour time slot. You should use it as your personal improvement hour, however, and not for time wasters, like catching up on one of your TV shows.

Another meaning on how the early bird really gets the worm, which I would like to share with you, is that you understand, by choosing to be proactive and taking action, you get your pick of whatever *worm* there is, rather than resorting to taking whatever is left. You will see examples of this all around you, except now, by reading this book, you will be fully conscious of them. Let's look at a couple of quick examples for you.

Leadership is for the Birds

Imagine you are in a line up at a buffet. Would you prefer to eat the food that was put there at the beginning, or what is left at the end, just before closing? It's still the same food; however, you would probably beg to differ in terms of the freshness between both time frames. At the beginning, it was just processed, whereas at the end, whatever is left may have been sitting there for some time because the owner doesn't want to cook more just before closing for the evening. Another example would be a certain sale that is limited in quantities, where you show up too late because others have taken action in order to reap the benefits of that specific sale and limited supply.

I will share with you a personal story. In my personal situation, time is so highly valuable that I will only work with those who are willing to take action. Sometimes I will have programs that are there for those who wish to transform themselves, to help them make it to the top. This can happen in various forms, and utilize different tools or strategies that will help you attain your goals. You will soon learn with me, however, that they are usually limited in supply. This is because I truly believe that if you are serious in wanting to make changes for yourself, that you will be that early bird that really gets the worm. I could work with so many more, but I choose to really concentrate on those who really want to make changes. These actions can only be decided by you. How bad do you really want what you want? You will not want to miss out on what I have to offer, and you should definitely take advantage of, at a minimum, subscribing to my email distribution list so as not to miss anything. That will take you about 15–20 seconds in order to do so. You can do so at www.LeadershipKing.com.

You can probably think of someone in your life who exemplifies taking action and going for it. If you ask them, you'll probably learn that they begin their day very early on, in order to gain a tactical advantage in tackling tasks that are the most important priority to them, and act with timely efficiency. As such, the person you are thinking of is probably very successful, and creates a positive, individual, and teamwork attitude, and is continuously at the top in whatever they do. Sometimes they are at the top in many things, all at the same time.

So, does the early bird really get the worm? Yes. You just have to decide what quality of worm you are looking for, and how much you are willing to fight for it, should you have competition. Yet this should never be an issue for you. The reason is that you end up making decisions where others will gravitate to you, allowing you to create a strong teamwork approach from all individuals, creating an environment where they will also do whatever it takes to be the first ones to help provide that worm for you, not because they have to, but because they want to.

Choose to be a leader, and take the accelerated steps to bring your goals into action. At the same time, help others also find their happiness in achieving their mission in life. If you help them achieve their dreams in life, they will give you the right to allow you to lead them. Earn their trust. Take action early on. At least, at a bare minimum, do something. This way, you will have results that are different than the status quo. By reading this book, and subscribing to my email list on my website, at www.LeadershipKing.com, you are not searching for status quo; for taking action, you will be exposed to many bonuses to help you continue your flight to success! For that, you should congratulate yourself, as you are taking the initiative to make changes for yourself and those around you.

Maximize Your Flight Plan

You will have probably noticed that I have made references to Canadian geese throughout this chapter. The reason is that you can learn so much from your surroundings, if you simply

Leadership is for the Birds

take the time to observe and be conscious of what is going on around you.

In other words, maximize your flight plan. Do as what the geese have shown you: migrate. In reference to the geese, the definition of migration refers to seasonal movement from one region to another. The Canadian geese fly south during the winter when they start to sense seasonal changes in their environment. Another way you can view migration is the movement from one part of something to another. Let's look at this together in more detail.

There are a couple of items that you will need to be aware of in order to fully maximize your flight plan. These are related to opportunities, changing environment, personal desire, and having a plan.

In regards to opportunities, these exist everywhere. If you are not satisfied or feel you have an opportunity where you physically are, move to an area that has opportunities. If you do not want to move, embark on opportunities that will allow you to take advantage of certain vehicles, such as the internet. Actually, when you subscribe to my email distribution list at www.LeadershipKing.com, you will be exposed to some of the latest internet opportunities that actually work. Making money online is an opportunity that anyone can do, if they are disciplined and follow the learnings that are taught. Since I didn't have these skills before, I needed to learn them from the best coaches and mentors in the industry, which you can do as well. Subscribe to my email list, and you will learn the secrets in making money online, as this is an additional strategy for you, to help you leverage earning income while you are following your deepest desires. Obviously I have to make a disclaimer that I cannot guarantee your success in regards to anything you do yet I will at least share the information. At this stage of where we are, if you are not making money online, you are already behind the curve. You will correct this quite quickly though, as you continue your journey with me. You see, you can move to areas of opportunities, you can create your own opportunities, or you can leverage opportunities on the internet that will allow you to communicate with anyone throughout the world! Maximize your opportunities that are around you!

In regards to changing environments, the world you live in today is nowhere near to what the world was 50 years ago. The world that you live in today is in hyper evolution. The skill sets that you have learned may be obsolete in the next couple of years. Ask any young person to have a good conversation (without using their Smartphone and texting), and you will be surprised in regards to their communication skills. You might feel uncomfortable knowing that is occurring, yet you know that it is also an opportunity to continuously learn other skill sets. Observe and analyze where the world is going, what new opportunities are being laid out, and stay ahead of the curve. Get interested! You are seeing more and more millionaires and billionaires than ever before, as people evolve quickly and plug into the evolution of things.

The next component is regarding your personal desire. This is controlled 100% by you. You decide how badly you want it. You have the choice to go through life being engaged at whatever level you want. It goes both ways though. If you have no personal desire to continuously improve and maximize your flight plan, you must accept the consequences that come about for the actions you take (or don't). You will most probably feel unfulfilled, yet that is your choice. No one will judge you for that, except yourself. However, since you made the choice to do so, you will understand that that is the flight plan that you have chosen. If that's where you are, and you are looking to change and transform yourself, keep reading this book. Be a part of my group, helping others transform their lives, including yours. Make that commitment today.

And last, but not least, make a plan. Think about it. You plan everything you need when you go on a vacation, right? Do the same thing for your deepest life desires. Your deepest desires are the most important things, which you cherish. If you do not have a plan, how are you going to maximize obtaining those desires? If you planned a trip to an island in the Caribbean, but the pilot flew you to the North Pole because he didn't have a flight plan, would you be happy? Of course not! You booked the plane ticket that would specifically bring you to your desired destination. This simple example shows you how important it is to have a plan to get exactly what you desire.

You have learned some interesting leadership concepts in this chapter, and it only gets better! In the next chapter, you will be going even further into learning some of the secrets of nature and how this applies to you. You will definitely not be able to put this book down because so many images, and a deep understanding on how this relates to you, will begin to pop up in your mind. It will excite you so much that you may also want to put some extra time aside to continue right through to the end of the book. Move to the next chapter right away!

Chapter 8

Nature's Patterned Secrets

"I'm a student of patterns. At heart, I'm a physicist. I look at everything in my life as trying to find the single equation, the theory of everything." – Will Smith

It's a Bird, It's a Plane, It's.....a Pattern?

....It's a pattern?

You probably have that bewildered look on your face, trying to figure out what that means to you. To answer this question, know that all the habits you exhibit are based and built from patterns. Now that you know this, you can take the necessary steps in order to do something about the habits you want to change, by changing your patterns. You will also note that the world functions on patterned habits. As such, most people behave in a predictable fashion. Let's look at a couple of examples so that you understand what this means.

Next time you're sitting in an airplane, prior to exiting the plane, note what people will automatically do. Immediately, more than half of the people in the airplane will stand up, and others will attempt to get their bags, while some will partially stand in an awkward position, with their head tilted sideways against the overhead compartments. Without a doubt, this happens all the time. Habit. Take a moment and picture this scenario: there is only one exit, and everyone is going to have to follow each other by structured rows, with the front rows first, followed by all the others rows afterwards, right? Even though this is the case, you will always see this pattern occur. Habit.

Another example is that of an elevator. This is a riot. First of all, you'll have certain people that will push the button over 100 times in 5 seconds. *Sir, or ma'am, the elevator will take you where you want to go, regardless of how many times you push the button after the initial pressing of it!* Yet they assume that pushing it 100 times will make it appear faster. Habit. They may acknowledge this after analyzing the situation, yet they will continue to do so, if they have not taken the time to acknowledge this and bring it into their conscious mind. You'll also find that when the elevator doors open, people waiting to get into the elevator will automatically try to enter it, without ever being conscious that there may be people wanting to exit the elevator first! Habit, habit, habit. Here is one final elevator example for you, because you're probably starting to get the point: you are standing there in the elevator, the doors are open, and someone is looking to get on. You say, "We're going up." Their response? "Oops, sorry, I didn't realize. I didn't look at the big, bright, flashing *Up Arrow* in front of me. Habit. Most times, nowadays, you will probably notice that they are looking at their smartphone as they say this to you.

Where is all this going?

Life, actions, decisions, behaviours, experiences, and so on, is all structured patterns that can be formed into becoming habits. In life, if you do the same things, every single day, in the same routine, at the same time, you are living a life of habit. This is not necessarily a bad thing, if that is what you are searching to do, or if these habitual actions are helping you achieve your ultimate goal (such as a fitness program). If you are unhappy with certain situations, however, or you find yourself complaining and choosing to play the victim, you will need to work on changing the attitudes and beliefs associated with what is creating your habitual behaviours.

Think about your ultimate dreams and desires. Are you taking action and creating patterns that turn into habits, which work towards your ultimate passion? If not, you need to make that change immediately, if you are really true to yourself in wanting to meet the needs of your deepest desires. You might be procrastinating, or you might be fearful, or you may have any other reason as to why you have not embarked on these actions. That being said, whatever the reason, you can definitely do it.

Here's an example for you that will put things into context for you.

Think back to when you first learned how to ride a bicycle. You were probably filled with so much fear, and never thought that you would ever master the skill. Then, you did! What a feeling! I can bet you, when you now get onto a bicycle, you don't think twice about being able to ride it. You see, you mastered the skill; through repetition, learning from your mistakes, and building your confidence, you unconsciously ride that bike now, without thinking about it.

Look at another example: Michael Jordan. He was probably one of the best basketball players to have ever played the game. He worked so hard on his game: he practiced and took so many shots every single day, that when it came time for competition, he had already lived the moment so often, and was running on automatic habits. You can do the same in regards to the actions you need to take, in order to fulfill your deepest desires in life.

Assembling the Assembly Line

You just learned what habit is all about. According to Oxford, it's "a settled or regular tendency or practice...a practice that is hard to give up...an addictive practice." Life is an amazing creation of multiple habits. In this section, you will learn how to assemble the assembly line.

When I present at seminars, some of you mention to me that there is nothing you can do because you are stuck in a mundane, repetitive lifestyle. Maybe you don't have enough time or money to do the things that you really want to do. It can be whatever reason or excuse you want to convince yourself of.

My response is always the same.

You brought yourself to that situation or place and time; therefore, you can bring yourself to another place in time, where you will prosper and be engaged in what you do. Find a way to leverage your own personal skills through someone you know who has those skills, and leverage experts who are doing it, if you can't or don't have the time to do it yourself. Learn how to assemble your own assembly line.

The assembly line is considered as one of the most influential and greatest innovations that took place in the 20th century. It so modified the industrial world that if businesses did not adjust and adopt these principles, they would be disadvantaged versus those who implemented them.

The most common example where this occurred, which probably immediately popped into your head, was in the automobile industry. Basically, prior to the assembly line, items were handcrafted by specific experts, and later brought together at the end, in order to complete the product.

The big change?

When businesses used interchangeable parts, and created standardization in the processes via an assembly line, output and efficiency to produce products, spiked. Henry Ford implemented the process, and was able to produce mass production of his vehicles at that time. Then, robotics came into play, optimizing efficiency, and working tirelessly around the clock, thereby eliminating jobs in the form of human capital. Then, the globalization era occurred, where businesses were installing factories where they could maximize their profits using certain tax advantages, cheaper labour, less expenses regarding functioning their factories, etc. Evolutionary changes began to accelerate tremendously.

You, as a proactive leader, need to assemble your assembly line. In your plan, there will be certain people who will save you ample amounts of time because they are experts in that area. Leverage your experts.

You have certain strengths. Leverage your own strengths. Make it known that you are an expert in this area. Negotiate your expertise, in exchange for someone else's expertise, in a different area that will help you attain your deepest desires.

The internet revolution that has occurred in the past 20 years is just in its infancy in regards to the potential solutions that it can provide to others, including yourself. If you are not leveraging an online, revenue-generating channel as part of your plan at the moment, I strongly suggest that you will need to do so immediately. This will provide you with income that will be generated at any time throughout the day (even when you're sleeping), in which the whole world has access to tap into. Very powerful. This is obviously important in that you are leveraging a system to produce income, all while you are focusing on your plan to attain your deepest desires.

In order to succeed with an online channel, you will need to learn what actually works; there are, unfortunately, certain things out there that don't. I will save you years of time, as I have already done all the research associated with this. As such, you will be able to quickly plug into this assembly line as part of your plan, and leverage this as well.

If you aren't jumping up and down by now, nothing will excite you! This is an unbelievable opportunity that I will be sharing for the first time, with the publication of my book. Remember, at a minimum, all it takes is 15–20 seconds. You simply need to subscribe as being a member of my email distribution list. You will understand as to why this is important, at a future time. Save www.LeadershipKing.com amongst your favourites!

Succeed with Speed from the Seed

Did you ever notice how small most things are at their initial stages, only to blossom fully, afterwards? Take something as small as a seed or, if you really want to get small, the size of a single sperm. Can you imagine that you became who you are in today's world, yet you were originally the size of a sperm? Think of all the growth, duplication, and nurturing you underwent from this tiny sperm and ovum, into becoming the person you are today. Your life is indeed a miracle.

The same can be said with any seed that is planted. It will follow its course of life but can be maximized in its success, if you are there to help guide its growth along the way. As you learned in a previous chapter, you can choose to nurture the seed, with vitamins, water, sunshine, etc. The only difference in this section is that, in today's world, you need to add the value of speed to succeed.

What does this mean?

It means, in order for you to take advantage of any evolution, you can no longer necessarily sit and wait before moving forward. Technology, globalization, and efficient systems are allowing people like you the opportunity to achieve success faster than any other time in the history of mankind. These facts alone are creating a separation amongst those who evolve rapidly, versus those who are trying to cling onto the status quo.

As a society, we are moving towards an environment that is based on speed and the breaking of barriers: high speed internet, bank machines, drive-thru, and so on. We live in a society of instant gratification, and as life thrusts you forward, you must be able to adjust and break your own barriers; that is, break your own habits of what used to work. You need to be cognizant in stopping the autopilot of the old, in order to program your autopilot of the new. This will allow you to take control of your plan of action and bring you closer to meeting your goals, desires, and dreams. It is better to decide than abide.

With a click of a button, you have access to an ample amount of information regarding pretty well any subject. You are living in a society that is seeing evolution occur almost instantaneously. One of the only areas that have not evolved to where it should be, is the current educational system. The process in teaching how we acquire knowledge in today's educational system is outdated and archaic to previous generations.

Since you have decided that you want to become a leadership king by polishing yourself right up to the top, you need to do things and take actions that are in line with today's society, as well as even to where the future is taking us. In other words, for you to succeed in however small steps you need to take, you need to do so with the utmost speed and efficiency.

Human Automation

This is a rather new area as to where the world is heading. You have already seen or experienced a revolution in regards to the robotics era. Basically, this is where robots or machines replace humans in regards to performing certain jobs or tasks. Maybe you underwent a downsizing experience and were replaced by a machine or robotic process.

Some will even say that the next revolution will be in regards to artificial intelligence. This means that intelligence will be displayed by machines rather than the natural intelligence that is displayed by humans and other animals. In other words, artificial intelligence is where a machine will mimic the cognitive functions of what humans associate with other humans in regards to areas of learning or problem solving. Therefore, the goal of artificial intelligence is to create technology that allows computers and machines to function in an intelligent manner.

You, on the other hand, have to learn the skills of human automation at the moment. In general, you basically make decisions in two different ways. The first way is that you take the time to analyze a situation, and try to use logic to figure out what decision you need to make at that specific moment in time. On the flip side, based on your experience and exposure in regards to certain situations, you can also make a decision based on intuition or gestalt. Human automation for today's world is the application of incorporating both of these ways of making decisions but at the same time.

You need to become a master of automating both logic and intuition together at the same time. Usually, analyzing a situation takes time and is a slow process, whereas acting on intuition is relatively not dependent on time. In essence, you will need to learn how to integrate humans, machines, and systems, to work together in such a way that the integration and interaction between all parties can be based on learned, unconscious, pattern-like recognition. That's a mouthful, so let's look at an example together.

Imagine that you are an experienced anesthesiologist. You are constantly given various vital signs from your patient, and you must decide whether or not to increase the dose of a drug to your patient, who is undergoing surgery, to be the most effective at that specific moment. On the one side, you have machines that are able to detect and provide you with information based on the vital signs of the patient. You also have your experience as an anesthesiologist, where you have learned different scenarios, through different surgeries throughout your lifetime, linked to certain actions that might be necessary to take, based on your feelings and previous experiences. Human automation would be the marriage of both of these sets of information, optimizing your decision-making, based on both, in the fastest, most efficient fashion possible.

In your quest for *transforming the coal in your soul to diamonds*, you must integrate and leverage the efficiencies of machines and software, along with your experience and knowledge. For areas in which you lack knowledge, you have access to ample amounts of information and experts throughout the world. Perhaps you think this sounds complicated, but you will see how this will integrate quite easily into helping you achieve your goals and desires in life.

For example, you are already learning leadership concepts from me in this book, but you will also learn applicable actions to take beyond this book, should you decide to do so. This will include having you plug into an online system to generate income in an automated fashion, while consciously working towards your personal goals. You will leverage and automate certain human actions.

What Would Darwin Think?

In the 1800s, Charles Darwin developed different theories based on biological evolution. The Darwinian Theory, in simplistic terms, states that the species of organisms arise and develop through the natural selection of small, inherited variations, which increase the individual's ability to compete, survive, and reproduce.

Why would you care to know what Darwin would think?

The fact of the matter is, because society is evolving at such a rapid rate, you need to evolve as a leader, and take actions to allow you the ability to compete, survive, and reproduce, regarding your specific goals, and this, in any era.

Think back to the automobile workers who are working on the assembly line. As robotics started to become mainstream, their roles and skill sets started to become obsolete. If you were one of those individuals who were downsized because of that, and you didn't prepare accordingly, you would have been left with the feeling of not knowing what to do or where to turn. Hence, you need to take an interest and learn where society is moving next, and how you fit within that transformation.

The exciting component for you is that you now know that only the strong survive when it comes to evolution. You may even note or observe that in today's workplace, more people are getting more done, with less and less available resources. This is not accidental, and is usually because companies are looking to maximize profitability.

Nature's Patterned Secrets

What about you?

How can you maximize what you want?

Learn to evolve. Understand that change is inevitable, so accept it. Take the initiative, and learn from it. Create your own destiny, your own results. Take the actions required today to plan for what is required in tomorrow's world. Those who stay on top of the wave of change are able to surf it rather than be engulfed and drown by it.

Do not assume that this always relates to job or income either. You may have the deepest desires to help underprivileged children gain an education. In order to do so, in a very simplistic approach, you will need to develop a plan that will provide strategic actions that will allow you to fulfill your deepest desires, to take actions and learnings, and evolve towards that goal. Rather than reinventing the wheel, use the wheels that are already created, and leverage your time with them to allow you the time to evolve with your utmost highest priorities to where you want to go, all done in the most efficient time possible.

Create Your Own Pattern

A pattern or template is something that you can use or create, which acts as a foundation so that it can, afterwards, be repeated in a predictable manner. You see this all the time: the patterns that you wear on your clothes are woven in a certain way; the repeated patterns displayed on certain wallpaper; or the same repetitive patterns you do every single day upon waking up. For example, you sleep on the same side of the bed, get dressed in the same fashion, brush your teeth the same way, etc. If you want to feel a change in regards to your automatic patterns, do the exact opposite in regards to all those things, for 1 day. In other words, sleep on the other side of the bed, brush your teeth with your other hand, and so on. You will experience a whole new feeling.

Almost everything you do is based on a predictable, pattern-like behaviour. Advertising companies, website cookies, and so on, are so targeted now, even when you search for information on the internet, the different sponsors associated in regards to your search will all of a sudden pop up within your pages. Where you are today is a reflection of the patterns and repetitive actions that you have taken throughout your life journey so far.

The natural order in the world is chaos. To demonstrate this, visualize taking a jar of marbles and putting a layer of white marbles on the bottom, followed by a layer of yellow marbles on top on those, followed by a layer of blue marbles on top of the yellow ones, and so on. Now, take the jar and shake it vigorously.

What happened?

You will note that the coloured marbles in the jar are chaotically distributed everywhere. The natural order in life is chaos and disorder. The only way that you will be able to quickly reposition the marbles, in their original form, is to manually interject and reposition them in their original pattern. The same goes for you.

You can chaotically go through life, without a plan, and never really achieve what you are specifically looking to achieve. You follow pattern-like behaviours all the time. Some of these are, of course, required in order to create a safe environment. An example of this would be traffic lights. Following the patterns displayed by street lights allows for order and safety throughout the world. If you choose not to follow certain patterns, such as going through a red light at a traffic light, the end result could be a horrible and deadly accident.

In relation to your transformation, this is where you create your own patterns. You know exactly what you want to achieve in life. Create the patterns required to access that! Take the actions needed, based on your thoughts and feelings, and attain those goals. If you don't know how to reach a certain aspect, ask someone who knows how. Every single action you take towards your goals all adds up to the pattern of life that you are trying to create for yourself.

You will learn, in the next chapter, that by creating your own patterns in life, you will be the captain responsible for your life ship! You will know the plan on how to get to your destination, and will navigate yourself accordingly. Don't wait. Jump on board to the next chapter, and see what is aboard your life ship!

Chapter 9

Captainship is Today's Leadership King

"There can be only one Captain to a Ship."
– Thomas John Barnardo

Captain + Ship = Captainship

The word, *captainship*, is not necessarily the most common word that you will hear people mention when you hear them talk about leadership. Actually, it is a very precise word; however, that defines specifically what you will need to do. As a definition, captainship refers to a position or command over a team, ship, or aircraft. If you know people who are serving their country in the United States, it is also utilized in regards to a certain ranking in different areas, such as the US Navy or the US Coast Guard, just to name a few examples.

In regards to how the word captainship refers to you, is that you are actually going to break the word into two words. Captain + Ship = Captainship.

Metaphorically speaking, you are the captain of your own ship. You decide what your ship looks like, how it is run, how many people work with you for it to function, where you are going, etc. You learned in previous chapters about assembling the assembly line; now, as captain of your own ship, you are overseeing all the different components that help your ship

Transform the Coal in your Soul to Diamonds

function to its utmost efficiency. In order to do so, you must learn and exhibit certain behaviours, or have certain attributes, in order to lead to the best of your abilities.

One of the most important characteristics that you must have is to be in total control of your emotions. Certain things may happen along the way, and remaining in total control of your emotions will allow you to make decisions that are logically based, at that specific moment. As you learned in regards to human automation, over time, your experience will also be utilized to make quick and necessary decisions. As captain of your ship, you must act when needed, especially if you see an iceberg in the waters ahead.

Another characteristic is that you are relentless in your actions. This simply means that you will do whatever it takes in order to achieve what you so deeply desire. Think about it. If your deepest desire is your ultimate goal in life, it is that priority that positions itself as the most crucial and most important to you. Be relentless in finding solutions, at all stages, to bring you closer to achieving this.

You must know and learn the rules of the game. Just as you maneuver your ship towards your destination, you must understand the rules associated in seamanship. The importance of that, to you, is that knowing the rules of the game allows you to play to the utmost limits of those rules. In other words, you are able to strategize accordingly, to maximize the ways to achieve your goals without crossing the boundaries and getting your ship stuck in shallow waters. Examples of breaking the rules would be manipulation, cheating, stealing, etc. Be a noble captain and steer clear of the temptation of shortcuts that will most of the time thrust you into a detour.

Another component, regarding your new role as captain, is to serve those around you. Perform your duties with pride, determination, and a sense of happiness in serving others around you. Sometimes this may involve decisions where you receive no recognition, although you know that your actions have made a difference to the greater good of others, and has helped guide your ship to the appropriate port, as flawlessly as possible.

First One On....Last One Off

It is interesting to note, as a captain of your ship, you should always be the first person on. Your ship is your responsibility. Most people view leadership in that fashion. You might think that the person in the front, taking charge, or the lead, when it comes to making decisions, must be the leader. The title of the chapter, *Captainship is today's leadership King*, indeed refers to that aspect of leadership, but also adds an extra component. The leader is also at the back. The leader, such as yourself, will remain to the bitter end, to ensure that no one is left behind. Basically, as a captain, you are the first one on your ship, and you will always be the last one off, regardless of any situation. Good or bad. You are responsible for your ship.

I want to share a wonderful story with you that took place many years ago, as the concept totally relates to your new responsibilities. Imagine for a moment that you go back in time, almost 500 years ago. It is the year, 1519, and you load up approximately 600 soldiers, approximately 16 horses, and lead your main ship in front of 11 others. You are going to Mexico...but not for a holiday!

You are going to Mexico in order to conquer an area full of treasures, which no one has ever been able to do for over the last 600 years. Oh, by the way, the other piece of information

Transform the Coal in your Soul to Diamonds

worthy of noting is that your army is also outnumbered by a 5:1 ratio.

What are the words you say to your troops?

You only say the following 3 words when you land onto the desired plateau in Mexico, and that's it: "Burn the Boats."

In other words, by taking such a bold action, you and your troops knew that they had 2 choices: die or ensure victory. The result? You successfully conquered Mexico.

The moral of this story is that the *burning of the boats* is all about your commitment to your strategy of attaining your deepest dreams, goals, and desires in life. It has to be such a priority to you that there is no turning back once you decide to commit to it. If what you were doing connects with you right down to your core, there is no reason to turn back. Your strategy is unique to you and your goals. No one else will do this for you. You must commit wholeheartedly to your journey, from start to finish.

You now understand the importance of all the different aspects you have read about so far, and on how each one is important for you at different steps within your journey. You are like a chef, creating a masterpiece with a certain recipe, knowing that each ingredient fulfills a certain role in its contribution to your creation. You are like a maestro, conducting an orchestra, and leading the different musicians to harmonize and embark at certain and appropriate times.

Be committed to your journey. It is yours. Own it.

Disciplined Responsibility

In order to achieve anything you want in life, you must display a certain amount of discipline. In essence, it is more like a disciplined responsibility since you are the responsible leader, ensuring that you hold everyone accountable for their actions, including yourself.

As a captain of your own vessel, it is the disciplinary actions you exercise that will guide a set of expectations to be met, or not. When you think about it, you may actually consider time management as being a form of disciplined responsibility. You basically utilize time as the requirement to be used efficiently. You collectively maximize the results of the disciplined responsibilities of each activity being completed within a certain time frame. In today's technological society, you are exposed to numerous tools, techniques, and software that will ensure that you, and anyone who is helping you achieve your goals, remains true to the time allotments that have been set out by you.

You will fully understand the importance of being disciplined in regards to your actions and strategies towards your goals. As you have already learned, you need to have a clear plan that is written, in order to guide you to where you and your ship want to end up at as a final destination. This plan will be ranked in priority in regards to tackling the most important tasks first. Therefore, you need to know where you want to end up and how much time it will take for you to get there. Once you determine that, work backwards and set timelines that are linked to the different strategies that are laid out, in order to achieve that final goal. For example, if you are on your ship, and the goal was to travel across the Pacific Ocean in 30 days, via Hawaii, then you should know exactly what time and what coordinates your vessel should be located at, throughout your journey. Obviously, there are certain situations that occur, even with the best planning, for which you must adjust your trajectory. That being said, your plan, as a *Captainship King,* should account for some sort of variability as part of your contingency plan, so you can, therefore, remain disciplined and be responsible with your approach, yet flexible to adjust to any unforeseen circumstances.

Did you ever notice that any gym is full of people for the first two weeks of January? Why is that?

Well, you've already learned that most people are predictable in their actions, so it should come to you as no surprise that the vast majority, or masses, make this New Year's resolution in regards to going to the gym and getting in shape. Usually, after approximately two weeks, attendance tends to drop quite dramatically, and only the truly committed remain; the reason being, most do not have a written plan as to what they are going to do, or as to how long it will take them to achieve their goals.

For many years, when I was a personal trainer, your first meeting with me, if you were my client, would have been an extra 30 minutes longer than the original meeting. The reason for this was to develop a targeted, time-driven, specific program that would meet and be tailored to you and your situation. You would also sign a commitment contract with me to ensure that you would be responsible and accountable for your actions. As your trainer, I ensured that you would be disciplined in following the plan that was laid out and created based to your specific needs. The reason for sharing this story is that you can utilize and leverage so many things in order to help you maintain discipline with your actions.

Trusting Confidence

In order to leverage different situations, and in order to achieve success, you'll have to learn how to build a trusting confidence in regards to those around you, as well as within yourself. Trust is a choice. It is something you choose that will make you vulnerable to other people, so be wise with your choice. That means, you have to have confidence that the people you surround yourself with have the greatest of intentions for you and your goals. There is a high level of love, partnership, and commitment involved in trusting someone.

Did you ever experience someone who has broken your trust?

Of course, you did. Everybody has, unfortunately, experienced that. You undergo a sea of emotions as you sit in your vessel of life, wondering why someone would ever break this ever-important bond. It hurts. So, it does take, and will take, a lot of time for you to fully trust someone to the core, but when done correctly, it is absolutely well worth it.

How can you really be certain to have trusting confidence with someone?

Nothing is for certain in the world we live in. You must do your ultimate best at building trust with a select few, and exemplify certain characteristics. These characteristics are within your full control, so building trust is driven quite heavily from you.

There are a couple of things you can do. First of all, you have to be open and fully transparent when you communicate with someone. Share your ideas honestly, and provide feedback to others with respect and sensitivity to how they view the world.

Transform the Coal in your Soul to Diamonds

You will notice, in doing so, that you will build a high level of trust, and others will fully appreciate your openness, even when there is a situation of contradiction.

Follow through on what you say. Be loyal to your words, and take responsibility for your own mistakes. Your statements mimic where your soul is, so be the person others can rely on. The promises and commitments you make need to be consistent and predictable in regards to your behaviour. People will have a connection with you, and build a trusting relationship, if they feel you are always consistent in what you do.

You don't necessarily know what other people have gone through in their journey of life. They may have undergone such negative experiences from others, that their ability to trust you may be hampered, for the simple reason that they have been burned too many times by others. You have to understand the mirror others project, and have the confidence that, over time, you may be the person that changes their views because you exhibited patience, flexibility, and tolerance in accepting them for who they are.

Be confident in yourself—even in the unknown—and have the confidence and trust that you will find an answer to continuously progress forward, in harmonic alignment to your goals. A word of caution for you: sometimes others will view your confidence as arrogance. In other words, if you display an overconfident behaviour, others might view you as cocky or arrogant. There is a fine-line difference between both, however, in that arrogance is unmerited, whereas confidence is deserved. Have a trusting self-confidence in your abilities since your intentions are pure and filled with love.

GPS Your Path

Think back to the last time you wanted to go on a trip, which consisted of driving to a location that you didn't know how to get to.

What did you do? How did you plan to get from point A to point B? Did you simply get into your car and drive, hoping that you would eventually get there by chance? Did you talk to someone who has already been there, in order to get directions? Did you look at a map? Did you do an internet map search to determine specifically how to get there?

You see, there are many different ways and tools that will help you get to your end destination. As long as you know where you want to end up, the processes that you utilize in order to get there, will vary from one person to another. In order to be a leadership king by polishing yourself right up to the top, you must choose a route that is the simplest, most efficient way of achieving your end result and desired outcomes.

GPS your own path. The letters, *GPS,* stand for global positioning system: it provides a geolocation and information in regards to time. In today's current society, GPS technology is so powerful that it can help guide you to your location of choice by taking other considerations into account, such as accidents, construction areas, etc., and calculate the time of all the other routes, to suggest to you the quickest, most efficient route. You need to act in the same way with your life—with your actions. GPS your own way to success!

Use your internal compass to point the needle in the right direction.

Transform the Coal in your Soul to Diamonds

Imagine a compass with no needle. How useful would this tool be to you if you were stranded and lost in the middle of a large forest? You would most probably agree that it would be useless.

How about a compass that has a needle that points to the north (assuming you are in the Northern Hemisphere)? Would that be useful?

You might be automatically tempted to say *yes,* immediately. Actually, that would be a normal response, because it's an automatic conditioned response, like many other things. However, it might not be useful. It's actually somewhat of a trick question, just to make you think. It might be useful in that you'll have some direction to follow; however, this may not be the direction you want to be following. For example, what if your car, or cottage, is located within a 5-minute walk, south of that point, and there is nothing north for over 100 kilometres?

Basically, this just shows you that you can have all the tools in the world to guide you, but the utmost important piece of information necessary, which these tools or GPS devices need to have, is that their use is modified in a way to help you achieve your specific goals. You have to make sure that your GPS, or internal compass, is pointing to the direction of your goals, not someone else's.

Captain's Crown

Most captains will wear captain hats. You, however, will wear a captain's crown throughout the rest of your journey, for numerous reasons.

First of all, you are working towards becoming a leadership king, in whatever goal that you have set for yourself. In this

Captainship is Today's Leadership King

respect, crowns are symbolic to kings. Another aspect is that *king* crowns are very highly valuable, as they are immersed with precious gems and diamonds throughout. As you transform yourself, from the coal in your soul to diamonds, you are polishing the valuable gems integrated within your own leadership king crown. You will also notice that my leadership king logo is on the back of this book. This logo will serve as a brand of excellence, in which you will crown yourself, onward, as we continue our journey together, even beyond this book, and also if you decide to purchase any of my official merchandise around this logo. Therefore, treasure your crown as you continue to sail towards your goals as a captain of your own ship.

Step out and take control of your final destination. You may have certain lighthouses, traffic controllers, or interference from others who are on the same CB frequency as your ship, etc., who will try to alter your path. Obviously, certain information is important, and change will need to occur. That's okay. An example of this would be the lighthouse indicating for you to alter your course of action; otherwise, you will hit the rocks on shore, and your ship will sink. Warning signs exist everywhere; it's just to make sure you listen to those who are there for your well-being, versus those who are there to set you off course, or distract you.

In my over 15 years of working in the pharmaceutical industry, there was a huge discrepancy on how to go about selling competitively or against competition. The different forms of doing so will each provide success in its own way, but is one way better than another? What I want you to learn today is that regardless of the model, the end result must always be that you find ways to create a valuable learning experience for those you interact with. Offer a captain's crown worth of value in regards to all actions you take.

Transform the Coal in your Soul to Diamonds

You should start to begin to feel a certain glow about you: an aura of preciousness; a powerful, loving, bright shining light that exudes from your presence; a sense of pride and honour—proud to be who you currently are, and of the contributions you are working towards making, moving forward.

You are almost at the end of the book, and just starting to embark on the start of your new life—your new transformation. A bright sparkle...

Do not stop and let this brightness fade. Continue onward, complete the reading of the next chapter, and shine bright!

Chapter 10

Shine Bright Like a Diamond

"You are, at this moment, standing, right in the middle of your own 'acres of diamonds'." – Earl Nightingale

Blissful Reflections

You should see yourself. Go take a look at your reflection in the mirror. You are nearing the end of this book, and getting ready to embark on a personal journey towards your success. See how you look and feel. Sense the emotions that are flowing within you at this moment. The reflection you see from yourself is pure bliss: a blissful reflection that shines bright.

Do you remember how you felt when you first started reading this book?

Do you already see the big changes in how you feel at this specific moment?

You have every right to be proud of yourself. If you didn't look at yourself in the mirror today, do it now. Really, take one minute, and smile at yourself in the mirror—for a complete minute. The sensation you will feel is a blissful appreciation of who you have become, in such a short period of time. The fact that you have almost read this book in its entirety will help you in leaps and bounds in regards to whatever project, action, behaviours, etc.

Transform the Coal in your Soul to Diamonds

that you take from the initial day you picked up my book, moving forward. You purchased my book for a reason, and you are acquiring your answers.

The exciting aspect in all of this is that you are just at the beginning of extracting the value of your internal diamonds. All the negativity, issues, and barriers that attempt to shunt your dreams are quickly dissipating away. The polishing glow, which you project, shines so strongly that it pierces the dark around, and illuminates wholeheartedly outwards. Let the shine, shine in.

Take a piece of paper and write out the following words: "I am a blissful reflection of my diamonds within." Make copies of this sentence and post it on your fridge, in your car, and on your bathroom mirror—anywhere and everywhere. Take a picture of the cover of my book, and save it as your wallpaper photo on your Smartphone, tablet, or computer screen—everywhere. By doing so, you are always taking the steps to continuously remind yourself of the happiness you feel for all the actions you are taking. Be proud. Love yourself. Share your learnings that you have received from me in this book, with others who you love. Buy them my book as a gift: a small contribution from a monetary point of view, with infinite value to them! You will help them to also achieve their personal dreams and desires.

I wish you could hear, feel, or even see a video of how I feel inside at this specific moment. This moment of connection with you is worth millions of *bliss coins* to me. Happy money. You have this wealth within you. Helping yourself attain what you truly, truly, truly want, will allow you to radiate as your own energy source.

You will look at this chapter of your life in a whole new light now. You probably didn't realize that your transformation was already well underway. I can confirm with you, it is. What you reflect outwardly will be so blissfully bright and blinding, that others will continuously ask you what your secret is to your happiness. Share this with them. Publicly express your life goal desires, and most will help you attain what you have planned to do. People want to be a part of something big—something that makes an impact in this lifetime. You are committed, so hold yourself accountable by stating this to others.

Glowing Rheostatic Intensity

You've probably seen or maybe even have, in your house, a light switch that is connected to a variable rheostat, which has a purpose in controlling the intensity of the lighting in that room. In essence, a rheostat is a variable resistor with the purpose of controlling current.

There will be times where you will need to control your actions, and the intensity, regarding your own internal goals. At certain moments of your life plan, you will need to increase the intensity of your internal rheostat, so that it is glowing with full luminosity. At other times, you will need to modify your rheostat, so your intensity matches according to the situation you're facing at that time. For example, you may have someone doing a specific task for you, which requires time. If this is a step that needs to be completed before you move on to another aspect of your journey, it does you no good to be fully intense with them at that specific moment. This only adds pressure to a situation that requires time as its variable to complete.

Another way of looking at your glowing rheostatic intensity is in regards to your desire for wanting to achieve your deepest life goals.

Are you a 1 on 10, on your dial? An 8?

Transform the Coal in your Soul to Diamonds

Maybe you are in full intensity mode, and you have yourself cranked up to the maximum, 10 on 10. Maybe you need changes in the circuits to allow for more energy. Whatever the case may be, you need to understand that you are the controller of your own internal rheostat. You gauge the intensity. You control the luminous glow. You are the electrician of your dial.

In today's world, the application of a rheostat doesn't really exist anymore in that switching electronics have really replaced them due to their low efficiency. However, when used as a variable resistance in circuits, it is used for tuning and calibration. To that extent, being in tune with your goals, and calibrating yourself with your aspirations, sets you up perfectly in deciding how much flow you need at a specific time.

Illuminate the diamonds that are within you, and allow them to glow. Allow the acres of diamonds within you to radiate. Commit to polishing them, as more come into play.

Symbol of Commitment

What is the first image that comes to your mind when you think of what the biggest symbol, attached to the meaning of commitment, is?

If you thought of a diamond ring, you would probably have many people that would agree with you. Usually, when one person is making a commitment to another person, they give them a diamond ring as a symbol of their love for their partner. Marriage: a symbolic union. The diamond ring also serves to convey a message to others that they are already committed to another person. In essence, the diamond ring reflects the values of the person wearing it, and serves as an outward, non-verbal message to others.

Shine Bright Like a Diamond

Take a look at what the word, *commitment*, means. Simply put, commitment is the state of being emotionally or intellectually devoted to a belief, an action, or even another person. In marriage, the contract is signed by both individuals as a commitment to their union together. With your life plan, the actions that you lay out in priority sequencing, with their timelines, are written so that you can move forward and commit to these.

Do you always have to have a diamond ring as the symbol of commitment?

Of course not. You can have anything you desire to represent your symbol of commitment.

This brings me to a story that one of my Jewish friends educated me on, which I was not aware existed. My friend was explaining to me parts of the Jewish practice. He then brought up the subject of how some Jewish people will wear what he called *phylacteries*. In case you don't know what those are (like I didn't know); they are small leather boxes that contain scrolls with scripture passages. Supposedly, some wear these phylacteries on the wrist during prayers, as it serves as a sign that they have internalized the Mandate of Shema (words that shape their living from my understanding). It is amazing to see how many different symbols exist in the world, and on how they have some association to commitment.

Other religions will wear certain necklaces or pendants, such as the cross, as symbols of faith, and reminders of the beliefs that they are committed to. It is absolutely interesting to read about and understand how all these different religions each have their own symbols that represent what commitment is all about. It also associates them to specific groups of people who share the same values.

The question you have to ask yourself is: "who, or what symbol, are you committed to?"

Propose to Yourself

You'll find that this statement of proposing to yourself has a lot of meaning and power behind it.

Proposing to yourself is the ultimate promise of commitment, which you are making to yourself in order to achieve any of your ambitions. You can view it as the union of your inner self and your outer self. Everything you feel and think about yourself *inside*, is committed to everything in regards to the actions you take with your *outside* self. Proposing to yourself means that you are loving yourself, and doing whatever it takes to heal all that is within.

Do you ever remember telling a secret to someone when you were young, and to ensure that they didn't tell anybody else, you made sure to do a pinky swear (locking of the pinky fingers)?

You may have noticed a new concept that is starting to pick up momentum more recently. Certain women are wearing what is being called *pinky rings*. In other words, it is jewelry that is worn on the pinky finger, displaying to others that they are committed to a certain specific cause that is personal to them. These pinky rings are linked to a specific pinky promise, which they have made to themselves, and have a declaration message that has a deep meaning to themselves. Whether you decide to wear a pinky ring as a symbol of your commitment, or not, do what is required to remain committed to yourself. Get married to yourself.

You'll probably notice that many people seek to get married with a significant other because this is what society has conditioned many people to follow. Maybe you are married to someone, or maybe you're not. In either situation, it is always your choice, and there is no wrong answer. As long as you love yourself, and are committed to everything that you represent for yourself, you will always be married.

I'm going to share a very personal story with you. Maybe you can relate to a similar story, and if that is the case, you will understand why I am sharing this with you at this stage. I was very fortunate to have had a wonderful relationship of over 19 years, with the mother of my two fabulous girls, who mean the absolute world to me, and will forever, for the rest of my life. Everything was aligned between the two of us, until she fell out of love with me, closer to the end of our years together as a couple. Although she contemplated staying together for the better of the kids, it was actually best that she left on her quest to try to find her happiness with someone else, which at that specific time, she was searching to find. My only request to my ex-spouse, when she left, was that we continue to fully raise our girls in complete love and harmony. To this day, we have both committed in full to the development of our 2 girls, and for that, I am very thankful, because they are both so very special to me.

On my end though, I was crushed. The world of love that I had given everything for, was shattered—unrepairable. At that moment, I felt like I was going through such dark times, that I was coughing profusely on the internal soot that the coal within my soul was forcing me to breathe.

Was I really being forced to breathe this?

Wait a second. I had a choice in all of this. Either I play the victim, or I make the choice to move forward. Like it always seems to be, timing is everything. One of my best men, whom I hadn't seen for a few years, was in town, and met me for supper.

Transform the Coal in your Soul to Diamonds

He took one look at me, and his first words to me were, "I don't know what the hell is going on, but you need to love yourself first, buddy." Wow. I needed to propose to myself. That is exactly what I did. That internal value of love for myself has never stopped rising in value since that divine intervention. As strange as it might sound, I lived a wonderful marriage, and I also lived a wonderful divorce.

I was able to quickly get remarried too. The only difference was that, this time, I proposed to myself. Then, I accepted to marry myself.

You are now experiencing my openness in reaching out to you. I am doing this so that I can help you increase your value for yourself, to the highest of heights, and for you to continuously break all barriers that are not allowing you to connect with your precious treasures within.

Infinite Value

If you ever try to think of what infinity looks like, or where it ends, it is impossible to describe. Something that is infinite has no boundaries, and as such, cannot be measured, even though you may often try to quantify what infinity means.

So, how does infinite value pertain to you?

Your internal values, wealth, and passions need to be of infinite value to you. The value is worth so much to you that it is never ending. Nor can it be measured. It is an abstract concept in your mind; even when you try to take a snapshot to describe it to yourself on how large of value it is to you, there is not a wide enough lens that exists to be able to capture your infinite value, whatsoever.

Take a look at the symbol of infinity. It is like taking the number 8, and laying it down horizontally. If you place your finger anywhere on the infinity symbol, and trace it, you can continue doing this exercise forever. It never ends. Something of infinite value is so much larger than life that you feel how big it is, even just thinking about it.

What about no value?

This is something that I noticed over the years, and once I share this with you, you will never forget it. Imagine you are watching TV, and you are browsing through the different channels. You come across the Weather Channel. You remember that you have an event outside today, and you want to see if the meteorologist will be forecasting any chance of precipitation.

Have you ever heard a meteorologist say that there is a 50% chance of precipitation?

Never! This is because *50% chance of precipitation* doesn't tell you anything. It has zero value. It can't be 50%, because it has be either above or below, in order to tell you some information as to whether it will rain or not! The same thing goes for when you ask someone how they feel, and they say, "So-so." Zero value. Automatic responses that are habitual in nature. You will hear this all the time around you.

Take a stand and strive for infinite value. At least you know what direction you are heading in, and you will continuously strive strongly in the direction of your goals.

Other people may look at you and judge you, or place a low value on the desires that are so deeply important to you. Just a reminder to you: those are opinions. Their opinions. It is

Transform the Coal in your Soul to Diamonds

important to put yourself in their shoes to view and understand their point of view. However, remember that the most important component is that you always return to finish observing your values through your lens, in order to make your decisions.

Infinite value, in reality, is a paradox in itself: most try to place a value on infinity, yet it can't really be measured, as it is abstract in nature. Allow the diamonds within you to shine infinitely in all directions, and your value will be unmeasurable!

Is it I'm-possible that d-I-AM-ond's are Forever?

Diamonds are forever. They're resilient, precious, valuable, and infinite, if you choose to allow them to shine from within you.

You probably heard the saying, or heard the song, *Diamonds Are a Girl's Best Friend*. Marilyn Monroe sang this song back in the 1950s. It was performed in the movie, *Moulin Rouge*, fifty years later. Many people have sung it over the years. In today's society, for you, right now, the title would be more along the lines of *Diamonds are Mankind's Best Friend*—the obvious reason being that internal diamonds exist for both men and women. It is not attached to any gender, race, religion, or any other societal statuses. It lies within your soul, simply waiting to be transformed, from the coal in your soul, to as many diamonds as you can create.

You have been exposed to a wealth of valuable knowledge throughout my book, and it feels like we have known each other for years. How efficient you are able to transform and polish your soul diamonds depends on how deeply passionate you are, and how badly you want to take action for yourself, as we have spoken about throughout my book.

Shine Bright Like a Diamond

The metamorphosis of life, and the evolution of the world, is occurring at a remarkably accelerated speed. If you are feeling a little overwhelmed, that is okay. You can always go back and reread my book in full, in order to fully comprehend the different teachings that are within it, to help you become a leadership king, by polishing yourself right up to the top.

Your transformation to success involves you taking action, and doesn't stop at the conclusion of this book. You will note that my website, www.LeadershipKing.com, was created as an extension so that we continuously partner together on your quest to achieving your ultimate goals. You even have access to bonuses that I have never released before. You will even be able to access downloads that will be practical to your development.

This book was written for you. It is about having you see, feel, smell, hear, and taste everything about your deepest desires, and taking action to achieve them. Only you can make that decision, though. My offer to continue to work with you, at the end of my book, still stands. Continue to take action with me, and your diamonds will shine forever.

This brings me to my subtitle, which is written in a very specific way. If you read it as a sentence, it will simply state, "Is it impossible that diamonds are forever?" My answer to you is that it IS possible that diamonds are forever....if you choose that they are.

Break down the word, *impossible*, to the following: **I'm possible**

Break down the word, *diamonds*, to the following: d-**I-AM**-onds

This **BOLD** statement should be loud and clear for you now.

Transform the Coal in your Soul to Diamonds

I'm-possible.....

I-AM......

Let's rewrite this last subtitle correctly.

I'M-POSSIBLE that d-**I-AM**-ond's are **forever**!

Actually, it IS possible that your diamonds are forever.

Take action and polish your way right up to the TOP! www.LeadershipKing.com

I look forward to seeing you there!

About the Author

Vince Labossiere lives on the South Shore of Montreal, CANADA, but is currently a Senior Sales Trainer, responsible for 4 different therapeutic areas for a large biopharmaceutical company in Toronto, CANADA, with global headquarters in Dublin, IRELAND.

The author is available for delivering keynote presentations to appropriate audiences, and for making appearances on television and radio stations, as well as some private consulting. For rates and availability, please contact the author directly at: leadershipking@leadershipking.com

To order more books, please visit:
www.amazon.com

To obtain your Exclusive Prestigious Leadership King Forever Membership, in my Private Group, and to continuously be exposed to accessing the latest up-to-date information, and numerous other bonuses, please visit:
www.LeadershipKing.com

Finally, if you have been inspired by this book, continue to take action. Be a leader, to and with others, so that you can also contribute in helping others transform the *coal,* that is trapped in their *soul*, to *diamonds*, and allow them to shine bright, like you!

Made in the USA
Columbia, SC
22 March 2018